Attempts to Be Many

Nara Bak   Jana Buch   Donja Nasseri
Arisa Purkpong   Anys Reimann   Theresa Weber

Attempts to Be Many

Julika Bosch und Katharina Klang

Die Gruppenausstellung *Attempts to Be Many* verknüpft Positionen junger Künstler*innen, die sich mit der Pluralität von Identitäten auseinandersetzen und aktuelle, internationale Diskurse um Race, Gender, Identität und Kollektivität verhandeln. Die Ausstellung entstand in enger Zusammenarbeit mit Studierenden und Absolvent*innen der Kunstakademie Düsseldorf, deren Werke persönliche Erfahrungen, Erlebnisse und Identitätsverständnisse ebenso wie kollektive Geschichtsverständnisse vereinen. Sie formulieren eine Auffassung von Identität, die in Pluralitäten, Ambivalenzen und Vernetzungen begründet ist. Darin rücken sie in die gedankliche Nähe der Vorstöße Édouard Glissants, dessen Betrachtungen von Globalisierung in einer Welt der Relationalität unsere Auffassungen von Kultur und Identität maßgeblich beeinflussen. Sein anhand der Vermischung von Kulturen und Sprache (Kreolisierung) entwickeltes Denken, das auf traumatischen Auseinandersetzungen einer pluralen, „vielverwurzelten", (post-)kolonialen Gesellschaft beruht, widerspricht den exklusiven, starren, europäsichen Identitätskonzepten in Nationalstaaten, die nur durch einen unbedingten Wunsch zur Vielfältigkeit und Verbindung ausgehebelt werden können. Dieser Gedanke bietet die Möglichkeit, sich auf die Wechselbeziehungen unserer Welt einzulassen und über inklusive Formen des Selbst zu reflektieren, die über den Gegensatz-Diskurs des Ichs und des Anderen hinausgehen. Die künstlerischen Positionen der Ausstellung werfen die damit verbundenen Fragestellungen auf: „Wie kann ich selber sein, ohne mich dem Anderen zu verschließen, und wie kann ich mich für den Anderen öffnen, ohne mich selbst zu verlieren?"[1]

Die Werke der Ausstellung erzielen diese Vielgestalt und Komplexität über die Methodik der Collage. Sie umfassen Papiercollage, Collage-Paintings, Fotocollage, Assemblage, installative Collage sowie Soundcollage und Videoschnitt. Dabei arbeiten die sechs Künstler*innen der Ausstellung mit Additionen, Umformulierungen, Rekontextualisierungen zu bzw. von Bildern, Symbolen und Erzählungen. Die Technik der Collage eignet sich für ihre Inhalte insbesondere, da sie sich aus der Omnipräsenz alltäglichen, visuellen Materials formiert. In ihren bildhaften und sprachbasierten Fragmenten, Gegenüberstellungen und Überlappungen ergeben sie hybride Deutungszusammenhänge, die für einen prozessualen Ansatz stehen, der assoziative und konkrete Bedeutungszusammenhänge einbezieht und alternative, plurale Lesarten ermöglicht. Im Hinblick auf identitätspolitische Fragestellungen und die Entscheidung, wie wir uns selbst wahrnehmen und darstellen möchten, eröffnet die Collage eine geeignete Methode, dynamische, kollektive Konzepte von Identitäten gegenüber starren Konstrukten der Fremdzuschreibung und ideologischer Eindimensionalität zu formulieren. Damit bewegen sich die Werke der Ausstellung jenseits der normativen Erzählungen einer hierarchischen, patriarchalischen, (post-)kolonialen Gesellschaft. Vielmehr ermöglichen sie Neuformulierungen von Körpererzählungen und erlernten Narrativen. Die in *Attempts to Be Many* vorgestellten Positionen verbinden die aktuellen gesellschaftlichen Diskurse mit historischen Bildtraditionen, mythologischen Konzepten und tradierten Erzählungen. In ihnen erscheinen Adaptionen und Überarbeitungen weiblicher und androgyner Figuren aus Mythen und Sagen wie Medusa und Arabimba, Pharaonen wie Hatschepsut und Echnaton, Gottheiten wie Ishtar und Personifikationen wie die Allegorie der Nacht, mit denen sie sich gegen misogyne, diskriminierende Darstellungsformen und Genderstereotype wenden.

Das über Einzelpersonen hinausreichende Verständnis von Kunstproduktion zeigte sich von Beginn der Vorbereitungen zur Ausstellung in einer bemerkenswerten Offenheit der Künstler*innen in der Zusammenarbeit. Wider die Idee eines isolierten

Künstler*innen-Ichs suchten sie Schnittstellen und Kooperationsmöglichkeiten. Diese Fähigkeit sich gegenseitig zu unterstützen und Kooperationen einzugehen ist insbesondere vor dem Hintergrund der aktuellen Pandemie und der eingeschränkten Sichtbarkeit sowie im Kontext von Vergabeprozessen von Stipendien und Preisen, die eine hierarchische Bewertungsstruktur bedingen und Konkurrenzgedanken schüren, von Bedeutung. Außerordentlich freuen wir uns, die Kulturwissenschaftlerin und Schriftstellerin Mithu Sanyal für einen Textbeitrag gewinnen zu können. Mit ihrem Roman *Identitti* hat sie wichtige Ansätze in Bezug auf öffentlichen Diskurs um Diskriminierung und Identitätspolitik geschaffen. Auch in diesem, persönlichen Zugang zur Ausstellung durchbricht sie identitätspolitische Regulierungsdiskurse, die in den Kategorien Herkunft, Ethnie, Religion oder Geschlechts verflachen und etabliert stattdessen ein Ich im Plural.

1 https://www.deutschlandfunk.de/das-kreolisierende-weltdenken-100.html Letzter Zugriff: 21.3.2022.

Attempts to Be Many

Julika Bosch and Katharina Klang

The group exhibition *Attempts to Be Many* combines works of young artists who are concerned with the plurality of identities and are involved in ongoing international discourses on race, gender, identity and collectivity. The exhibition was conceived in close collaboration with students and graduates of the Kunstakademie Düsseldorf whose works incorporate personal experiences, perceptions and understandings of identites, alongside collective concepts of history. They formulate an understanding of identity based on pluralities, ambivalences and interconnections. In this sense, their approach converges with the ideas of Édouard Glissant, whose reflections on globalization in a world of relationality have had a decisive influence on our conceptions of culture and identity. His thinking, developed from the mixing of cultures and language (creolization), is grounded in the traumatic struggles of a plural, "multi-rooted", (post-)colonial society. It contests the exclusive, rigid European identity concepts of nation states and suggests that the latter can only be undermined by an unconditional desire for diversity and connection. This notion makes the engaging with the interrelationships of our world and reflecting on inclusive forms of the self that seek to go beyond the given oppositional discourse of the self versus the other possible. The positions presented in the exhibition raise the related questions: "How can I be myself without closing myself off to the other, and how can I open myself to the other without losing myself?"[1]

The works in the exhibition achieve their diversity and complexity through the methodology of collage; they comprise paper collage, collage paintings, photo collage, assemblage, installation collage, sound collage and video editing. The six artists participating in the show work with additions to or reformulations and recontextualizations of images, symbols and narratives. Drawing from the omnipresence of everyday visual material, the technique of collage is particularly suitable for the chosen contents. With their image–and language-based fragments, juxtapositions and overlaps, variegated collages produce hybrid contexts of interpretation: they stand for a process-oriented approach involving associative and concrete contexts of meaning and facilitating alternative, plural readings. With regard to questions of identity politics and the decision on how we want to perceive and present ourselves, collage offers suitable methods for articulating dynamic, collective concepts of identities, as opposed to rigid constructs of foreign ascription and ideological one-dimensionality. The featured works thus move beyond the normative narratives of a hierarchical, patriarchal, (post-)colonial society. Instead, they enable reformulations of body narratives and learned narratives. The positions presented in *Attempts to Be Many* link current social discourses with historical pictorial traditions, mythological concepts and traditional narratives. Adaptations and reworkings of female and androgynous figures from myths and sagas like Medusa and Arabimba, pharaohs like Hatshepsut, Akhenaten, deities like Ishtar and personifications like the Allegory of Night appear in them, challenging misogynous, discriminatory forms of representation and gender stereotypes.

From the beginning of the preparations for the exhibition, the artists' understanding of an art production that extends beyond individuals became evident in their remarkable openness to collaboration. Counter the idea of an isolated artist ego, they sought possibilities for exchange and cooperation. This ability to support each other and collaborate is particularly important against the backdrop of the current pandemic and limited visibility, and in the context of grant and award processes, which impose a hierarchical evaluation structure and encourage competition. We are extremely pleased to have gained the cultural studies scholar and writer Mithu Sanyal for a text contribution. With her novel *Identitti*, she has introduced important approaches to public discourse on discrimination and identity politics. In this distinctively personal approach to the exhibition, she once more disrupts regulatory identity-political discourses caught in the categories of origin, ethnicity, religion or gender and instead establishes an I in the plural.

1 https://www.deutschlandfunk.de/das-kreolisierende-weltdenken-100.html, last accessed: 21 March 2022.

Ein Versuch in drei Akten

Mithu Sanyal

Attempts to Be Many. Bäm! Einmal den Titel gehört und sofort gewusst, diese Ausstellung muss ich sehen! Wie werden wir *viele*? Wie werden wir mehr als nur eine abgetrennte Einheit, die isoliert von anderen existiert?

Aber auch, wie werden wir Gemeinschaft, ohne uns darin aufzulösen?

Let me explain: Wenn ich eine Google-Bildersuche (andere Suchmaschinen sind selbstverständlich genauso irritierend) starte und dort „Deutsche Menschen“ eingebe, erhalte ich *weiße* Deutsche, *weiße* Deutsche, *weiße* Deutsche ... irgendwann kommt Donald Trump (weil er ein Problem mit der Deutschen Bank hat) ... und erst viel viel viel später kommen die ersten BIPoCs, postmigrantischen Deutschen oder welche Bezeichnung bis dieser Text gedruckt ist gerade die angemessenste ist.

Wir sind in dem deutschen *wir* vielleicht mitgemeint, aber nicht mitgedacht.

Und dann passierte das Verblüffende: Nachdem ich diese Geschichte bei Lesungen und im Feuilleton erzählt hatte, erschienen plötzlich unter den ersten 25 Treffern: Walter Benjamin und Hans Sarpei und ich (mit einem Artikel über eben dieses Thema). Wenn es möglich ist, den Algorithmus von Google zu knacken, dann können wir noch ganz andere Narrative verändern: Attempts to Be Many!

Der Philosoph und Ökonom Amartya Sen hat dafür den Capability-Ansatz geprägt als Indikator für den Entwicklungsstand einer Gesellschaft, neben Bruttosozialprodukt, Bildung und Gesundheit. Der Capability-Ansatz misst, ob Menschen die Fähigkeiten haben, „die Dinge zu tun, die wertvoll für sie sind – sowohl individuell als auch als soziale Wesen – und dazu gehört Teilhabe am gesellschaftlichen Prozess, an öffentlichen Auseinandersetzungen, Werte zu teilen und Sorgen zu teilen.“[1]

Und Erinnerungen zu teilen …

Erinnern …
Doch wer ist in den Geschichten und Mustern enthalten, mit denen wir als Gesellschaft aus unserer Vergangenheit Fiktionen bilden? Und wie strukturieren diese Geschichten wiederum unseren Blick auf die Vergangenheit? Arbeiten wie die von Arisa Purkpong und Jana Buch machen die Erinnerungsfetzen und Überlappungen sichtbar, die Brüche und Risse in den linearen Erinnerungserzählungen. Ein kleiner Exkurs: Menschen können Informationen nur verarbeiten, indem wir sie in Sinnzusammenhänge stellen: wir narrativieren. Das ist erstmal eine gute Sache, die Welt besteht für uns aus Geschichten, alles hängt mit allem zusammen und alles macht (irgendwie) Sinn. Allerdings, erklärt der Neurobiologe Bruce E. Wexler, dreht sich, sobald die internen Strukturen des Gehirns einmal etabliert sind, das Verhältnis zwischen dem Inneren und dem Äußeren um. Nun werden unsere inneren Strukturen nicht mehr durch unsere Umwelt geformt, sondern wir beginnen Informationen zu ignorieren oder zu vergessen, wenn sie nicht mit unseren inneren Storys übereinstimmen. Weil Informationen von uns zu Geschichten verwandelt werden, *bevor* sie unser Bewusstsein erreichen. Individuell ebenso wie kollektiv. Deshalb ist die Frage, wer Teil der Erinnerungskultur ist, so zentral. Nicht nur: Wer ist *wir*? Sondern:

Wer erzählt, was *wir* alles sein können?
Und was *wir* alles gewesen sind …
Um wen trauern *wir*? …
Und worum trauern *wir*?

Trauer …
„Ich habe Menschen, die asiatisch gelesen werden, gefragt, ob sie ihre Erfahrungen mit Rassismus und Sexismus mit uns teilen, und dann haben Jana Buch, Jihye Lee und ich daraus eine Trauerrede geschrieben. So entstand dieses ‚Trauercafé'", erklärt Nara Bak und bietet Kuchen und Früchte aus Ton an, während im Halbkreis um diesen ungenießbaren Leichenschmaus Kerzen aus Porträts stehen, von denen stets zwei wie ewige Lichter brennen, so dass das Wachs wie Tränen von den Gesichtern tropft.

Trauer ist eine besondere Form der Erinnerung, sie ist die Brücke, die diese mit jener anderen Welt verbindet. In ihr liegt die Erinnerung an alles Jenseitige. Auch an die Zukunft. Und was ist mit der Erinnerung an die Zeit, bevor wir *wir* wurden?

Deep time …
Konzentrierte Memory-Fragmente …
Mythologische Zeit …

Deshalb ist es nur passend, dass Donja Nasseri in ihrem Raum auf Menschen zurückgreift, die zu ihren Lebzeiten bereits zu Mythen wurden: Auf Echnaton und Hatschepsut mit ihren uneindeutigen Geschlechtsmerkmalen. Sex und Power. Ikonen.

Glamour …
Auch Jana Buch und Arisa Purkpong beschäftigen sich mit Gender und Gewalt in Legenden: Mit Arabimba, die ihre Geschlechtsteile in einen Baum legt, oder mit Medusa, die in ein Monster verwandelt wird, damit sie von einem Helden umgebracht werden kann.

Haare wie lebendige Schlangen …
Fetisch …
Plateauschuhe und künstliche Fingernägel …

Als ich die künstlichen Fingernägel sehe, die sich wie ein Refrain durch die Arbeiten von Theresa Weber ziehen – eine immer weiter variierte Wiederholung – muss ich an den Mann denken, der mich einmal heiß umworben hat, und dann einen Rückzieher machte, weil ich lange Fingernägel habe und das für ihn ein No-Go bei Frauen ist. Ich war verblüfft von dieser doch sehr spezifischen Aversion, bis mir klar wurde, dass Fingernägel immer auch ein Zeichen von Klasse sind. „Mädchen ihrer Klasse haben normalerweise absolute Klauen," sagt Miss Marple in einem Agatha-Christie-Krimi über die Leiche einer jungen Frau und kommt zu dem Urteil: „Definitely not a lady".

Überhaupt geht es, je tiefer ich in die Ausstellung vordringe, um so mehr ans Eingemachte. Anys Reimann, die einen *Schwarzen Garten* in den White Cube des Museums gepflanzt hat, untersucht in ihren Collagen und Gemälden moderne Legenden, Ikonen der Leinwand, Stars und solche, die es hätten werden sollen: „Dieses Bild ist eine Hommage an den Film ‚Le Noir de…' von 1966, an die Frau, die darin die Hauptrolle spielt. Sie geht von Senegal nach Frankreich, um für eine *weiße* Familie zu arbeiten, aber ist dort vollkommen isoliert. Letztlich bin ich da drin, meine Gefühle zu diesem Film. Da ich nie in Afrika war …" – ein Satz, der mich mitten ins Herz trifft. Ich habe so viele Freund*innen, die so viel häufiger in Indien waren als ich. Trotzdem ist Indien in mir. Ist es das? Ja, aber was heißt das?

Fragmente, die nicht zusammengehören und sich dann zu etwas Neuem zusammenfügen. In dieser Ausstellung verwandelt sich etwas in etwas anderes. Wir kennen Glamour heute hauptsächlich aus dem Bereich der Werbung und der Celebrities. Dabei ist *Glamour* ein altes Wort für Zauberei, und zwar für Zauberei, die etwas mit Worten und Bedeutung zu tun hat. *Glamour* kommt von derselben Wortwurzel wie *grammar* (und wie das französische Wort *grimoire*, das ein Buch mit Zaubersprüchen bezeichnete). Eine Ausstellung mit der Macht, Begierden in Bedeutung zu verwandeln, Erinnerung in Gemeinschaft und Risse in Öffnungen: *Attempts to Be Many*.

1 https://www.youtube.com/watch?v=EN5esbvAt-w, abgerufen am: 10.02.2022.

An Attempt in Three Acts

Mithu Sanyal

Attempts to Be Many. Bam! I heard the title and instantly knew I had to see this exhibition! How do we become *many*? How do we become more than just a separate entity that exists in isolation from others?

But also, how do we become a community without being dissolved into it?

Let me explain: if I start a Google image search (of course, other search engines are just as irritating) and enter "German people", I get *white* Germans, *white* Germans, *white* Germans ... and at some point, Donald Trump appears (because he has a problem with Deutsche Bank) ... and only much, much, much later come the first BIPoCs, post-migrant Germans or whatever term is most appropriate until this text is in print.

Though the German *we* may also mean us, we are not included in thought.

And then the most amazing thing happened: after I had told this story at readings and in the feuilleton, suddenly among the first 25 hits appeared Walter Benjamin, Hans Sarpei and me (with an article on this very topic). If it is possible to crack Google's algorithm, then we surely can change completely different narratives: attempts to be many!

For this purpose, the philosopher and economist Amartya Sen introduced the capability approach as an indicator of a society's level of development, alongside gross national product, education and health. The capability approach measures whether people have the abilities "to do the things that are valuable to them – both individually and as social beings – and this includes participating in the social process, in public disputes, sharing values and sharing concerns".[1]

And sharing memories …

Remembrance …

Yet who is included in the stories and patterns from which we as a society concoct fictions of our past? And how, in turn, do these stories structure our view of the past? Works such as those by Arisa Purkpong and Jana Buch make specific memory fragments and overlaps visible – the fractures and cracks in the linear narratives of memory. A small digression: humans can only process information by embedding it in contexts of meaning – we narrativize. Which for a start is a good thing; we perceive the world as consisting of stories, everything is connected to everything else and everything makes sense (somehow). However, as neurobiologist Bruce E. Wexler explains, once the internal structures of the brain are established, the relationship between the internal and the external is reversed. Now, instead of our internal structures being shaped by our environment, we begin to ignore or forget information if it does not match our internal stories. Because information is transformed into stories by us even before it reaches our consciousness. Individually as well as collectively. That is why the question of who is part of the culture of remembrance is so central. Not only: Who is *we*? But: Who tells us what *we* can be?

And what *we* have all been …
Who are *we* mourning? …
And what are *we* mourning for?

Mourning …

"I asked people who are read as Asian to share their experiences of racism and sexism, and based on these Jana Buch, Jihye Lee and I wrote a mourning speech. That's how this 'mourning café' came about," explains Nara Bak, offering cakes and fruits made of clay, while arranged in a semicircle around this inedible funeral feast are candles made of portraits, two of which always burn like eternal lights, so that the wax drips from their faces like tears.

Mourning is a special form of commemoration; it is the bridge that connects this world with that other world, the hereafter. In it lies the memory of everything beyond. Including the future. And what about the memory of the time before we became *we*?

Deep time …
Concentrated memory fragments …
Mythological time …

So, it seems only fitting that Donja Nasseri, in her space, draws on people who already became myths during their lifetimes: Akhenaten and Hatshepsut with their ambiguous sexual characteristics. Sex and power. Icons.

Glamour …

Jana Buch and Arisa Purkpong are also concerned with gender and violence in legends: with Arabimba who places her private parts in a tree, or with Medusa who is transformed into a monster so that she can be killed by a hero.

Hair like living snakes …
Fetish …
Platform shoes and artificial fingernails …

When I see the artificial fingernails running like a refrain through Theresa Weber's works – an ever-varying repetition – I have to think of the man who once hotly courted me and then backed out because I have long fingernails and that is a no-go for him with women. I was taken aback by this very specific aversion, until I realized that fingernails are always a sign of class. "Girls of her class usually have absolute claws," says Miss Marple in an Agatha Christie mystery about the corpse of a young woman and comes to the conclusion: "Definitely not a lady."

In fact, the deeper I venture into the exhibition, the more I become engaged. In her collages and paintings, Anys Reimann – who has planted a *Black Garden* in the museum's white cube – examines modern legends, icons of the silver screen, stars and those who should have become stars: "This painting is a tribute to the 1966 film 'Le Noir de…', to the woman who plays the main role in it. She leaves Senegal and goes to France to work for a white family, but is completely isolated there. Ultimately, I am right in there, my feelings about that film. Never having been to Africa …" – a sentence that pierced my heart. I have so many friends who have been to India so much more than I have. Yet India is in me. Is it? Yes, but what does that mean?

Fragments that do not belong together and then, nonetheless, coalesce into something new. In this exhibition, something transforms into something else. We know glamour today mainly from the realm of advertising and celebrities. Yet *glamour* is an old word for magic, a kind of magic that has something to do with words and meaning. *Glamour* comes from the same root as *grammar* (and as the French word *grimoire*, which meant a book of spells). An exhibition with the power to transform desires into meaning, memory into community and cracks into openings: *Attempts to Be Many*.

1 https://www.youtube.com/watch?v=EN5esbvAt-w, accessed on 10 February 2022.

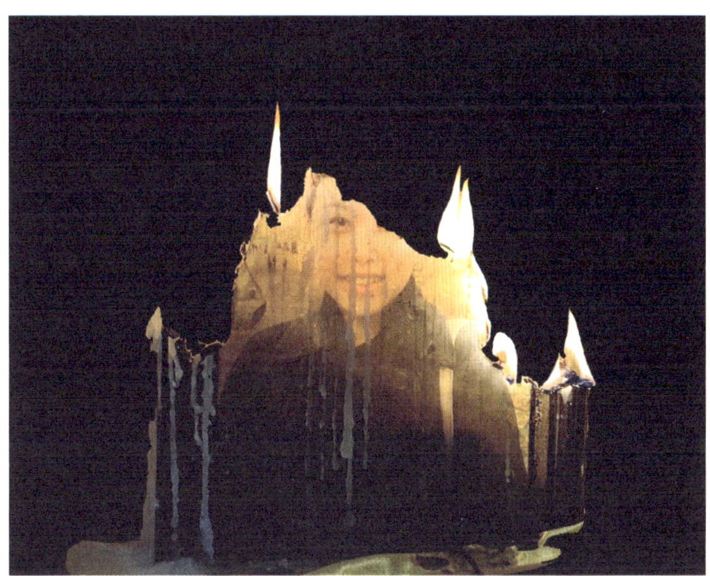

Trauercafé
2021

Nara Bak

Ausgangspunkt der künstlerischen Arbeit von Nara Bak (*1993) bilden eigene und gesammelte Aufzeichnungen, Empfindungen und subjektive Erfahrungsräume, die durch materielle Elemente und symbolische Repräsentanten erzählt werden. Für die Ausstellung in der Sammlung Philara hat Bak ein fiktives *Trauercafé* erschaffen.

In dunkler Atmosphäre können Besuchende an drei runden, weiß eingedeckten Tischen Platz nehmen. Die Szenerie wird von einem Halbkreis aus brennenden Kerzen beleuchtet, die während der Laufzeit der Ausstellung langsam abbrennen. Es handelt sich dabei um zehn Wachsporträts von Menschen, die aufgrund ihres Aussehens als „asiatisch" gelesen werden und während der Pandemie verstärkt Ablehnung aufgrund von Vorurteilen und anti-asiatischem Rassismus erfahren mussten. Ihre Erlebnisse sind die Grundlage für eine im Kollektiv entwickelte Soundarbeit, die in diesem Raum zu hören ist. Basierend auf Erfahrungen von Areumbit Park, Seoyoung Yun, Jung Yun Jang, Arisa Purkpong, Kyounghyun Min, Eunbi Oh, Lauraine Mak, Laude Yu, Yuni Hwang, Chaelin Jeon mit Rassismus und Sexismus, schrieb Nara Bak gemeinsam mit den Künstlerinnen Jana Buch und Jihye Lee eine Trauerrede. Der Sound der Trauerrede wurde gemeinsam mit Arisa Purkpong entwickelt. Auf Deutsch, Koreanisch und Englisch wird darin der symbolische Tod einer Freundin durch die Stimmen von Elena Packhäuser, Nara Bak, Jana Buch und Jihye Lee betrauert. Dazu wird von Performer*innen ein Stück Kuchen gereicht. Nara Bak behandelt mit dieser persönlichen Ansprache und in der dramaturgischen Aufbereitung koreanischer und deutscher Trauerrituale, die kollektive Tragweite von seelischen Verletzungen durch die ständige Wiederkehr von Mikroaggressionen und verbalen Angriffen, die in diskriminierenden Rassismuserfahrungen ihren Ausdruck finden. Die Arbeit verweigert sich bewusst anekdotischer Erlebnisse und betont an deren Stelle die verschwimmende Grenze des Selbst und des Gegenübers. Das Erzählen im „wir" durch die Künstler*innen ist geprägt von dem Wunsch nach Resilienz gegenüber seelischem Schmerz und dem Wagnis, sich in geistig offene Räume zu begeben, die sich jenseits von Schubladen-Denken bewegen:

Räume, die von empathischen Veränderbarkeiten, gedanklicher Flexibilität und freundschaftlichen Beziehungen geprägt sind.

Starting point for the artistic work of Nara Bak (b. 1993) is their own and collected recordings, sensations and subjective spaces of experience, which are narrated through material elements and symbolic representatives. For the exhibition in the Philara Collection, Bak has created a fictitious *Trauercafé* (Mourning Café).

In a sombre atmosphere, visitors may take a seat at three round tables set in white. The scenery is illuminated by a semicircle of lit candles slowly burning down over the duration of the exhibition. They consist of ten wax portraits of people who, in view of their appearance, are read as "Asian" and have felt a sense of increased rejection during the pandemic due to prejudice and anti-Asian racism. Their experiences are the basis for a collectively developed sound work that can be heard within the space. Based on experiences with racism and sexism shared by Areumbit Park, Seoyoung Yun, Jung Yun Jang, Arisa Purkpong, Kyounghyun Min, Eunbi Oh, Lauraine Mak, Laude Yu, Yuni Hwang and Chaelin Jeon, Nara Bak wrote a eulogy together with artists Jana Buch and Jihye Lee. The sound of the mourning speech was developed together with Arisa Purkpong. In German, Korean and English, the symbolic death of a friend is mourned with the voices of Elena Packhäuser, Nara Bak, Jana Buch and Jihye Lee, while pieces of cake are served by the performers. With this personal address and dramaturgical processing of Korean and German mourning rituals, Nara Bak deals with the collective scope of psychological injuries through the constant recurrence of micro aggressions and verbal attacks finding expression in discriminatory experiences of racism. The work deliberately refuses anecdotal experiences and rather underlines the blurring boundary between the self and the other. The artists' narration in the "we" form is marked by a desire for resilience in the face of mental pain and a willingness to risk entering mentally open spaces beyond stereotypical thinking: spaces that are characterized by empathic changeability, flexibility of thinking and friendly relationships.

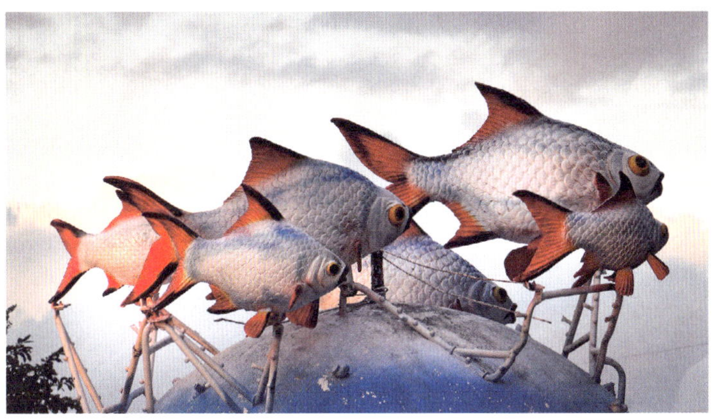

Notizen aus Stein (Filmstill)
2020

Jana Buch

Jana Buchs (*1988) interdisziplinäre, kollaborative Auseinandersetzungen umkreisen Sprache in kurzen Prosatexten ebenso wie in Fotografien. Ihre projektübergreifende Arbeit – eine filmische Kooperation mit Arisa Purkpong – schafft eine Verbindung zu der Sound-Collage von Nara Bak. Zudem sind diese beiden Werke dialogisch im Ausstellungsraum geschaltet: Mit dem Ende des Sounds des *Trauercafés* setzt die Videoarbeit *Notizen aus Stein* ein. Die von Jana Buch gewählte, assoziative, poetische Sprache beider Werke erzeugt eine starke Intimität. Die Künstlerin entwickelt ihre Texte nach intensiver Analyse, die sie mit einer ausgeprägten Aufmerksamkeit gegenüber verletzenden Narrativen verarbeitet.

Das Video *Notizen aus Stein* und die zugehörige Publikation entwickelte Jana Buch gemeinsam mit Arisa Purkpong. Darin führen die Künstlerinnen die Betrachtenden auf eine zeitliche, räumliche und lyrische Reise, die auf zwei tradierten Erzählungen basiert. Sie collagieren die Geschichten von Medusa und Arabimba miteinander: Medusa ist in der griechischen Mythologie die einzig sterbliche, dabei aber schönste von drei Schwestern. Sie wird häufig als männermordendes Ungetüm dargestellt – jedoch wird sie aufgrund einer Vergewaltigung durch Poseidon von der Göttin Athene mit einem Fluch belegt, durch den sie Schlangen als Haare trägt und jeden, der sie erblickt, versteinert.

Die Figur Arabimba entspringt hingegen einer jahrhundertealten buddhistischen Sage aus dem süd- und südostasiatischen Raum die ins Thailändische überliefert wurde und dort aus den Paññāsa Jātaka (50 Geschichten aus Buddhas vergangenen Leben) bekannt ist. Darin wird Arabimba von ihrem Mann Pacitta getrennt und verwandelt sich in einen Mönch, bis sie wieder auf ihn treffen kann. In diesem Prozess legt sie der Sage nach ihre weiblich konnotierten Attribute (ihre Brüste und ihr Geschlecht) ab, bis sie erneut auf Pacitta trifft. In der Gegenüberstellung der beiden Figuren machen die Künstlerinnen auf den ungewöhnlichen Umgang der beiden Frauenfiguren mit Leid sowie den Narrativen, die sie umgeben, deutlich: Während die griechische Mythenfigur sexualisierte Stigmatisierung, Gewalt und Tötung erfährt, entledigt sich die thailändische Sagenfigur ihrer biologischen Merkmale, um zu überleben. Besonders in Bezug auf die Narrative um Medusa fallen dabei die lange Tradition zutiefst misogyner Inhalte und die endlos scheinenden Bemühungen, sich dieser zu entledigen, auf.

Jana Buch's (b. 1988) interdisciplinary, collaborative explorations revolve around language in the form of short prose texts and in photographs. Her cross-project work – a film-based collaboration with Arisa Purkpong – creates a link to the sound collage by Nara Bak. In addition, these two works are set in dialogue in the exhibition space: with the end of the sound from the *Trauercafé* (Mourning Café), the video work *Notizen aus Stein* (Notes of Stone) begins. The associative, poetic language Jana Buch has chosen for both works creates a strong intimacy. The artist develops her texts after intensive analysis, which she processes with a keen attention to hurtful narratives.

Jana Buch developed the video *Notizen aus Stein* (Notes of Stone) and the accompanying publication together with Arisa Purkpong. The artists lead the viewer on a temporal, spatial and lyrical journey based on two traditional narratives. They create a collage from the stories of Medusa and Arabimba: in Greek mythology, Medusa is the only mortal, yet the most beautiful of three sisters. She is often portrayed as a man-killing monster – but because she was raped by Poseidon, she is cursed by the goddess Athena to wear snakes for hair and petrify anyone who sees her.

The figure of Arabimba, on the other hand, originates from a centuries-old Buddhist legend from South and Southeast Asia that has been passed down into Thai and is known there from the

Paññāsa Jātaka (50 stories of the Buddha's past lives). According to the legend, Arabimba is separated from her husband Pacitta and transforms into a monk until she can meet him again. In this process, she sheds her attributes with a feminine connotation (her breasts and her sex) until she meets Pacitta again. By juxtaposing these two female figures the artists point out the unusual way they both deal with suffering and highlight the narratives that surround them: while the figure in the Greek myth experiences sexualised stigmatization, violence and killing, the Thai myth figure rids herself of her biological characteristics in order to survive. Particularly in relation to the narratives surrounding Medusa, the long tradition of deeply misogynistic content and the seemingly endless efforts to get rid of it are striking.

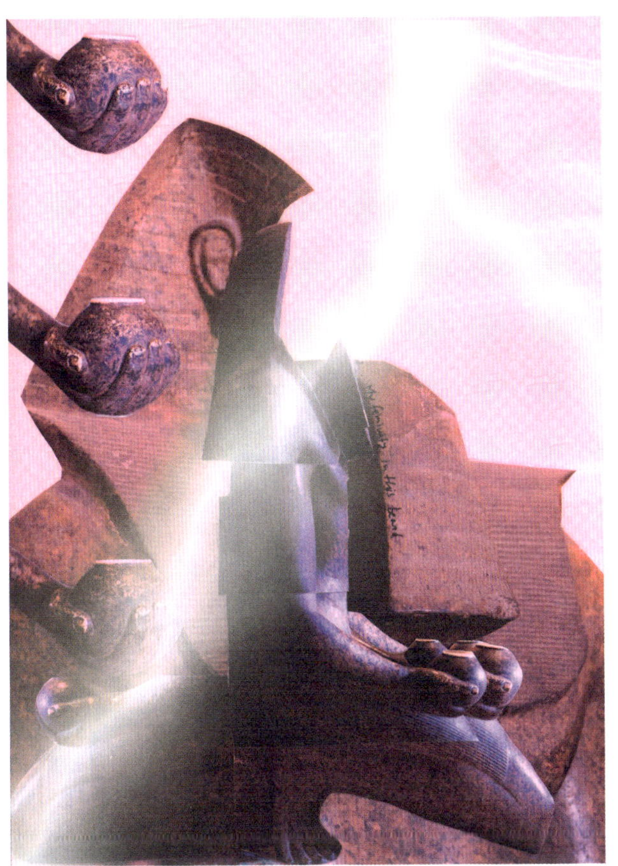

Femininity Photography
2021

Donja Nasseri

Donja Nasseri (*1990) widmet sich in ihrer aktuellen Werkserie fotografischen Collagen, die sie im Rückgriff auf Darstellungen von zwei prominenten Herrschenden des Alten Ägyptens einer queerfeministischen Analyse unterzieht. Unter Einbeziehung analoger und digitaler Techniken entwickelte Donja Nasseri für die Ausstellung *Attempts to Be Many* eine Serie von fotografischen Collagen sowie eine großformatige Deckencollage auf Textil. Der Pharao Echnaton war ein ägyptischer König der 18. Dynastie (14. Jh. v. Chr.). In den überlieferten, skulpturalen Darstellungen vereint er Aspekte, die sowohl als männlich als auch als weiblich gelesen werden können. In der archäologischen Rezeption werden die Körperzüge des Regierenden, etwa sein gerundeter Bauch und sein feminisiertes Gesicht, als weiblich beschrieben, was zu zahlreichen Theorien über seine nicht binär zuordenbare Körperlichkeit führte. Die Pharaonin Hatschepsut, eine der wenigen Frauen auf dem ägyptischen Thron (15. Jh. v. Chr.), ist der 18. Dynastie zuzuordnen und wurde mit männlichen Attributen dargestellt – beispielsweise mit angesetztem Bart. Die Darstellung folgt somit einer als männlich zugeschriebenen Ikonografie und Machtlegitimation.

In langer Recherche sammelte Donja Nasseri Abbildungen dieser körperlichen Merkmale und Symbole, die keine eindeutige Lesbarkeit zulassen. Dabei fotografierte sie Fragmente von Statuen im Ägyptischen Museum in Kairo und griff auf die umfassenden Online-Archive der Sammlung des Metropolitan Museum of Art in New York zurück. Im Anschluss beschnitt, collagierte, ergänzte und faltete Donja Nasseri das ausgedruckte, fotografische Material. In den Faltungen werden auch die Rückseiten der Fotografien sichtbar, die sie handschriftlich mit archäologischen und kunsthistorischen Zuschreibungen, geschlechtlichen Fixierungsversuchen und eigenen Notizen ergänzt hat. Manche der Fotografien wurden von ihr mit Nägeln durchstoßen und erneut abfotografiert, um Konzepte geschlechtlicher Eindimensionalität zu dekonstruieren und dynamische Vorstellungen von Identität zu formulieren. Die Verwendung von Nägeln ist nicht ausschließlich ein Rückgriff auf Methoden des Zusammenhaltens und des Ausstellens in Museen mit altägyptischer Kunst und Artefakten, sondern auch ein Kommentar auf den Akt der historischen Zuschreibung und Fixierung.

Donja Nasseri (b. 1990) has devoted her current series of works to photographic collages which she submits to a queer-feminist analysis by drawing on depictions of two prominent rulers of Ancient Egypt. Using both analogue and digital techniques, Nasseri developed a series of photographic collages and a large-format ceiling collage on textile for the exhibition *Attempts to Be Many*. Pharaoh Akhenaten was an Egyptian king of the Eighteenth Dynasty (14th century BC). In surviving sculptural representations, he incorporates aspects that can be read as both male and female. In archaeological reception, the ruler's physical features, such as his rounded belly and feminized face, have been described as feminine. This led to many theories about his physique as corresponding to a non-binary identity. The pharaoh Hatshepsut, one of the few women on the Egyptian throne (15th century BC) who belonged to the Eighteenth Dynasty, was portrayed with masculine characteristics, for instance, with an attached beard. The depiction thus follows an iconography and legitimization of power predominantly attributed as male.

In lenghty research, Donja Nasseri collected images of such physical features and symbols not permitting a clear reading. She photographed fragments of statues in the Egyptian Museum in Cairo and accessed the extensive online archives of the collection of the Metropolitan Museum of Art in New York. Donja Nasseri then trimmed, collaged, supplemented and folded the printed photographic material. The folds also reveal the backs of the photographs to which she added handwritten archaeological and art historical ascriptions, attempts at gender fixation and her own notes. She pierced some of the photographs with nails and photographed them again to deconstruct concepts of gendered one-dimensionality and formulate dynamic notions of identity. The use of nails is thus not exclusively a recourse to methods of holding together and displaying in museums with ancient Egyptian art and artefacts, but also a commentary on the act of historical attribution and fixation.

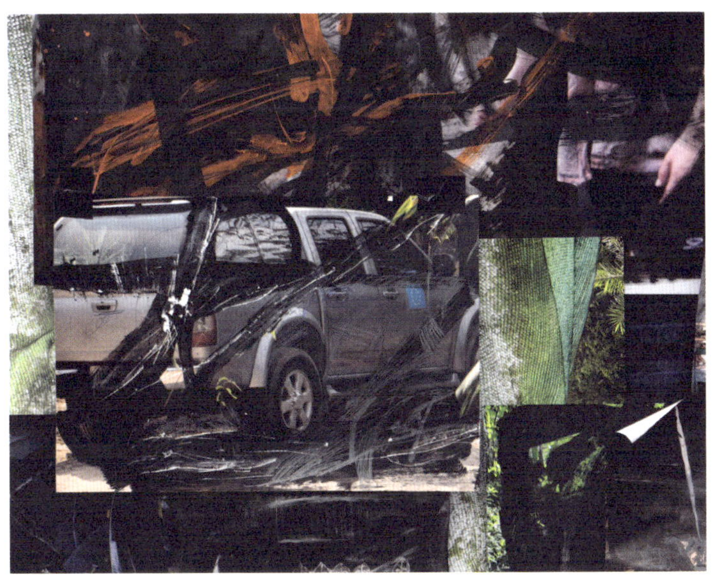

Ohne Titel (Detail)
2021

Arisa Purkpong

Arisa Purkpong (*1995) arbeitet von der Fotografie ausgehend in unterschiedlichen Medien, die sie miteinander kombiniert. Beispielsweise überträgt sie die Collage in die Installation und erweitert diese kontinuierlich. Für die Ausstellung *Attempts to Be Many* hat Arisa Purkpong eine solche raumgreifende und im Vorlauf zur Ausstellung stetig anwachsende Collage entwickelt. Etwa 4000 Fotografien wurden von der Künstlerin gesichtet, rund die Hälfte dieser wurden übermalt, zerknüllt, zerrissen, zerkratzt, übersprüht und einander überlappend im Raum installiert.

Die Fotografien basieren unter anderem auf persönlichen Auseinandersetzungen mit der feministischen, thailändischen Organisation *Friends of Women Foundation*, deren Ziel es ist, Frauen* in diversen, mitunter strukturell benachteiligten Gemeinden durch eine handwerkliche Ausbildung eine wirtschaftlich selbständige Absicherung zu ermöglichen.

Durch den prozessualen Ansatz der Künstlerin erneuert und schafft sie subjektive wie kollektive Erinnerungsbilder, die Verhaltenscodices, geschlechtliche Rollenzuschreibungen sowie unbewusst wirkende Narrative beschreiben und rekontextualisieren. Ihre gefilterten und selektierten Erinnerungen öffnen sich so hinsichtlich weiterer Assoziationen und Anknüpfungspunkte. Es entsteht ein großes Beziehungsnetz einzelner fotografischer Bilder, die ein Spektrum sich gegenseitig überdeckender, konkurrierender und rekonstruierender Momentaufnahmen und malerischer Gesten bilden. Darüber hinaus sind auch Textpassagen in der Collage enthalten. Es sind Spuren von gemeinschaftlichen Korrekturprozessen, auf denen die Arbeiten *Notizen aus Stein* und *Trauercafé* basieren. Das Handeln im Kollektiv, beziehungsweise die Zusammenarbeit mit Nara Bak und Jana Buch wird somit dokumentiert. Mit der Geste des Übermalens und des Überlappens eignet sich die Künstlerin eine Technik zur Aufbereitung erstarrter Darstellungen und verloren gegangener Erinnerungen an. In ihnen wird das Bild vielmehr zum Gegenstand von Flexibilität und Verhandlung kollektiver Prozesse. Rechts neben der Collage-Installation findet sich, im Ausblick durch ein Baugerüst, das die Künstlerin für die Konstruktion der Collage verwendet hat, eine weitere, aber einzeln präsentierte und großformatige Fotografie. Sie eröffnet eine neue Frage, die mit der Aufmerksamkeit jenseits des Zentrums der Erinnerung verbunden ist und mit dem, was an ihren Rändern oder parallel zu ihnen geschehen mag. Damit wird Erinnerung als prozessuales Konstrukt zwischen Ordnung und Entropie sichtbar.

Departing from photography, Arisa Purkpong (b. 1995) works across a range of media that she combines with each other. She transfers collage into an installation, for example, and then continually expands it. For the exhibition *Attempts to Be Many*, Arisa Purkpong has developed such a spatially expansive collage which, in the run-up to the exhibition, is constantly growing. The artist sifted through some 4000 photographs, about half of which were painted over, crumpled, torn, scratched, sprayed over and installed in the space overlapping one another.

The photographs are based primarily on personal encounters with the Thai feminist organisation *Friends of Women Foundation*, whose aim is to enable women* in various, sometimes structurally disadvantaged communities to achieve economic independence through training in handicrafts.

With her process-based approach the artist creates renewed images of subjective and collective memory, aimed at describing and recontextualizing codes of behaviour, gender role attributions and narratives effective on the subconscious level. The filtered and selected memories encourage further associations and points of connection. The result is a large interrelational network of individual photographic images, a broad spectrum of mutually overlapping, competing and reconstructive snapshots and painterly gestures. In addition, passages of text are included in the collage: traces from the collective processes of correction underlying the works *Notizen aus Stein* (Notes from Stone) and *Trauercafé* (Mourning Café). A collective action – the collaboration with Nara Bak and Jana Buch – has thus been documented. With this gesture of overpainting and overlaying, the artist has adopted a technique for reprocessing solidified representations and lost memories. Here, the image, as subject matter of the negotiation of collective processes, instead offers flexibility. To the right of the collage installation, in a view through scaffolding, which the artist used in order to construct the collage, one sees another photograph. A large format presented separately. It gives rise to a different question, one concerning our attention beyond the center of memory and what may be happening at its edges or parallel to it. Memory thus becomes visible as a processual construct between order and entropy.

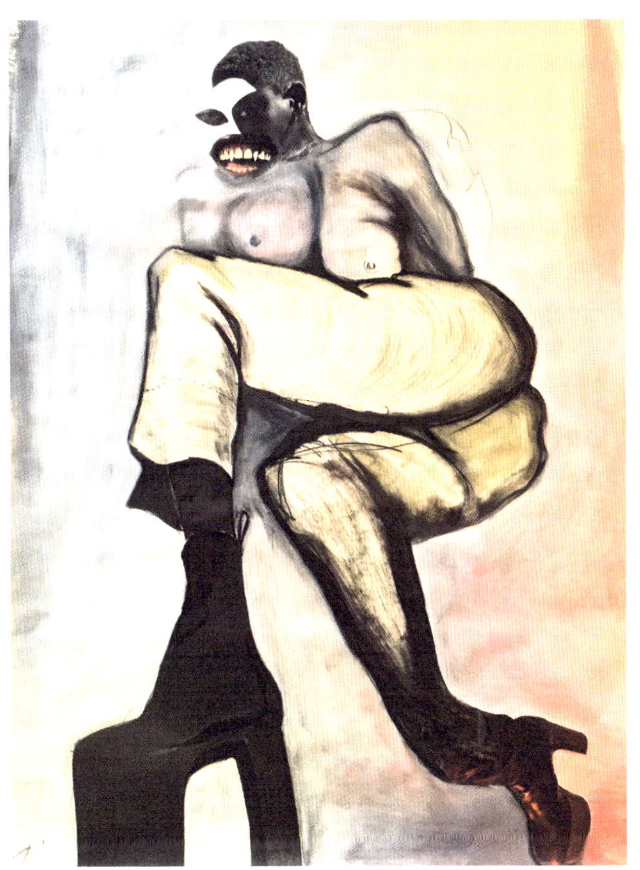

BLACK PLATEAU
2020

Anys Reimann

Die bildhaften und skulpturalen Arbeiten von Anys Reimann (*1965) vertreten Positionen von Emanzipation und Intimität in Bezug auf Identität, Race und Gender. In ihren Collagen und Collagepaintings wird ein hybrides und fluides Identitätsverständnis sichtbar. Sie arbeitet mit „found footage“ aus Kunst, Musik und Pop, die in collagierten und gemalten Schichten ineinandergreifen, um neue Sinnzusammenhänge jenseits von klar definierten Zuschreibungen herzustellen. In den Werken *LE NOIR DE... I – III* und *Die Nacht* kombiniert Anys Reimann einzelne oder mehrfache Gesichtsmerkmale, Organe und Körperteile zu hybriden Figuren. Letzteres zeigt beispielsweise die lässig rauchende Hand eines Künstlers mit dem Steintorso der Allegorie der Nacht im Medici-Grabmal von Michelangelo und den anmutig übereinander geschlagenen Beinen Marlene Dietrichs. Während Collage und Malerei hier stets Verbindungen eingehen, besteht das Selbstbildnis *Ohne Titel (a Self)* aus nur einer Bildseite, aus der das Gesicht so herausgeschnitten wurde, dass die Hautfarbe darin nicht mehr erkennbar ist. Wird das Werk an die Wand gehängt, nimmt das Porträt die dahinter liegende Wandfarbe als Hautfarbe an. Damit stellt das Selbstporträt auch die Frage nach der Vielzahl von Identitäten, die immer auch für ein Framing anfällig sind oder von einem solchen neu konstituiert werden. In ihrer Installation *Schwarzer Garten* hat Anys Reimann schwarz anmutende Callas, Alocasias, Anthurien und Heucheras in ein künstliches Beet im Ausstellungsraum gepflanzt. Der weiße Raum entspricht den gängigen Parametern des Ausstellens im Sinne des „White Cube“, dessen vermeintliche Neutralität immer wieder angezweifelt wurde, insbesondere vor dem Hintergrund aktueller politischer Diskurse, beispielsweise um die Sichtbarkeit und Bewertung von Black Culture im musealen Kontext. Im Vorlauf der Ausstellung hat sich Anys Reimann mit der US-amerikanischen Autorin und Yale-Professorin Claudia Rankine beschäftigt, die in ihrem Gedichtband *Citizen: An American Lyric* und in ihrer Publikation *Just Us: An American Conversation* weiße Privilegien und Orte untersucht, die eine geringe Diversität aufweisen, wie beispielsweise Tennisplätze. Anys Reimanns *Schwarzer Garten* übersetzt diese

Auseinandersetzung Rankines in den Ausstellungskontext und verweist auf diese konstruierten „unbewohnbaren Momente", die mit Beschränkung und Diskriminierung verbunden sind.

Anys Reimann's (b. 1965) pictorial and sculptural works adopt attitudes of emancipation and intimacy in relation to identity, race and gender. Her collages and collage paintings convey a hybrid and fluid understanding of identity. She works with found footage from art, music and pop, merging in collaged and painted layers that take on new meanings in new contexts, beyond clearly defined ascriptions. In the works *LE NOIRDE ... I–III* and *Die Nacht* (The Night), Anys Reimann combines individual or multiple facial features, organs and body parts to create hybrid figures. The latter, for instance, shows an artist's hand casually smoking, together with the stone torso of the allegory of Night in Michelangelo's Medici tomb and Marlene Dietrich's gracefully crossed legs. While, here, collage and painting forge connections, the self-portrait *Untitled (a Self)* consists of only one page from which the face has been cut out in such a way that the skin colour is no longer recognizable. When the work is hung on the wall, the portrait takes on the colour of the wall behind it as its skin colour. The self-portrait thus also addresses issues concerning the multiplicity of identities – which are invariably susceptible to framing or newly constituted by such framing. In her installation *Schwarzer Garten* (Black Garden), Anys Reimann has planted black-looking callas, alocasias, anthuriums and heucheras in an artificial flower bed in the exhibition space. The white room corresponds to standard parameters of presentation in the sense of the "white cube", whose alleged neutrality has been questioned time and again, especially in light of the backdrop of current political discourses, about the visibility and evaluation of black culture in the museum context, for example. Previous to the exhibition, Anys Reimann dealt with US author and Yale professor Claudia Rankine, who in her poetry collection *Citizen: An American Lyric* and in her publication *Just Us: An American Conversation* examines white privilege and places showing low diversity, such as tennis courts. Anys Reimann's *Schwarzer Garten* (Black Garden) translates Rankine's investigation into the exhibition context, referencing such constructed "uninhabitable moments" associated with restriction and discrimination.

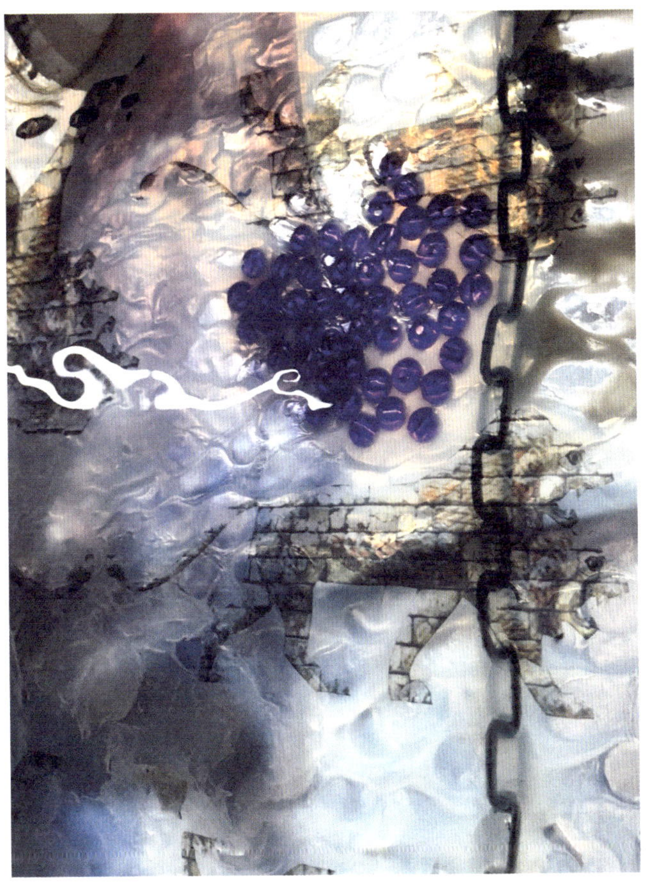

Transformation Gate (Detail)
2021

Theresa Weber

Theresa Webers (*1996) Werke formieren sich aus künstlichen Materialien, die eine identitätsstiftende Funktion übernehmen. In ihren Assemblagen verarbeitet sie Körperpolster, künstliche Fingernägel, Silikon, geflochtene Haarteile sowie Deko- und Bastelelemente, die nicht nur die Erweiterung des Körpers markieren und ein Selbstbild konstituieren, sondern auch Auskunft über soziale Zugehörigkeit, Gestaltungs- und Geltungsbereiche geben.

Auf zwei Bildträgern werden bunte künstliche Fingernägel neben und auf geformtes Silikon zu Landschaften angeordnet, die sich den starren metrischen Systemen westlicher Kartographie, und der Logik kolonialer Vermessungen widersetzen. Stattdessen orientieren sie sich an freien, kartographischen Darstellungen, die Informationen als Synthesen verhandeln. Die dahinter gelagerte, großformatige Wandtapete *Ishtar Wallpaper* verdichtet in rhythmisierenden, vertikalen Reihungen Bilder in einer Collagetechnik zu einem Flechtornament. Die Arbeit verbindet Darstellungen von Selfies der Künstlerin mit bildlichen Repräsentationen der mesopotamischen Gottheit Ishtar, die vermeintlich gegensätzliche Pole, das Weibliche und das Männliche sowie Fruchtbarkeit und Stärke in sich vereint. Das aus Babylon stammende Ishtar-Tor (6 Jh. v. Chr.) wurde Anfang des 20. Jahrhunderts von der Deutschen Orient-Gesellschaft ins Berliner Pergamonmuseum gebracht und steht im Zusammenhang mit der Debatte um Restitutionsverfahren. Für *Attempts to Be Many* hat Theresa Weber eine Installation mit dem Titel *Transformation Gate* entwickelt, die die Architektur eines Tors nachempfindet. Aus frei im Raum hängenden Modulen – Assemblagen auf lichtdurchlässigen Transparentfolien –, die durch hinausragende Haarteile und Ketten miteinander verbunden sind, entsteht ein mehransichtiges, visuelles Geflecht, das man durchschreiten kann. Theresa Weber verwendet auch hier künstliche Fingernägel und Haarteile, die zu Braids geflochten sind und verweist auf Materialien und Techniken, die für die Künstlerin eine empowernde Funktion übernehmen.

Theresa Weber's (b. 1996) works are composed of artificial materials meant to take on an identity-forming function. In her assemblages, she works with body pads, artificial fingernails, silicone, braided hairpieces as well as decorative and handicraft elements that not only mark the extension of the body and constitute a self-image, but also provide information about social belonging and areas of social design and validity.

Arranged on two supports, colourful artificial fingernails are next to and on moulded silicone to form landscapes defying rigid metric systems of Western cartography and the logics of colonial surveys. Instead, they are oriented towards free, cartographic representations that negotiate information as syntheses. *Ishtar Wallpaper*, the large-scale wallpaper situated behind, condenses images into a braided ornament in rhythmic, vertical rows using a collage technique. The work combines images of the artist's selfies with depictions of the Mesopotamian deity Ishtar, known for uniting supposedly opposing poles, the feminine and the masculine, as well as fertility and strength. The Ishtar Gate (6th century BC), which originated in Babylon, was brought to the Pergamon Museum in Berlin by the Deutsche Orient-Gesellschaft (German Oriental Society) at the beginning of the 20th century and is currently related to the debate on restitution proceedings. For *Attempts to Be Many*, Theresa Weber has developed an installation entitled *Transformation Gate*. Adopting the architecture of a gate, modules suspended freely in the space – assemblages on translucent foils – connected to each other by protruding hairpieces and chains fuse into a multi-perspective visual meshwork that one can walk through. Here too, Theresa Weber uses artificial fingernails and strands of braided hair, indicating materials and techniques that for the artist assume an empowering function.

Zwei Bilder

Text von Jana Buch

Die Form verdichtet sich
Glutheiß und fließend.
In der Linken das Haupt.
Im Blick der Stolz

Zielgerichtete Blicke
zeichnen ein Schema des Duplikats
Der Geist des Meisters Griff
formte einst haargenau.

Augen und Hände
formen die Körper
den Körper
ohne …

Negativ und Positiv
in einem Erguss.
Die Feinheiten sind nun verloren.
– „Stimmt"

Brachiale Umarmung.
Schnitt und Schuss mittendurch.
Die allerhöchsten Götter
schauen auf mich herab.

Übersetzungsfehler
einer Sprache ohne Laut.
Sie kennt nur Gesten
Ich höre sie dennoch jeden Tag.

Ich ahne
Ich weiß
Ich warne
Ich …

Mein Wille
hängt am Baum
wie meine Brust
– ich hole sie später wieder ab.

สองภาพ

Text von Jana Buch
Übersetzt von Sarah Herndon und Jana Buch

รูปร่างบีบอัดก่อตัว
ของเหลวหนืดเหนียว
ศีรษะไร้ร่างในมือซ้าย
แววตาเขาภาคภูมิ

การจ้องมองของเขามุ่งมาด
กวาดร่างแนวคิดของร่างแฝดคู่ขนาน
สัมผัสประณีตของครูศิลป์
รังสรรค์เส้นผมคดเคี้ยวของหญิงสาว

ดวงตาและฝ่ามือ
ปั้นแต่งเรือนร่าง
ร่างกายที่
ปราศจาก…

เปลือกนอกและเนื้อใน
การหล่อหลั่งเพียงครั้งเดียว
ชะล้างทุกรายละเอียด
“ใช่Ó

สวมกอดรัดรึงแน่นขนัด
ฟาดฟันทะลุถึงใจกลาง
พระองค์เจ้าผู้สูงส่ง
ปรายตามองข้าจากเบื้องบน

คำแปลที่ผิดพลาด
ของภาษาไร้สุ้มเสียง
มีเพียงการเคลื่อนไหวล่องหน
ที่ข้ายังได้ยินมันอยู่ทุกวัน

ข้ารู้สึกได้
ข้าทราบดี
ข้าได้กล่าวเตือนแล้ว
ข้า…

เจตนารมณ์ของข้า
ขึงแขวนไว้บนไม้ใหญ่
เช่นเดียวกับทรวงอก
แล้วข้าจะกลับมารับมัน

Two Images

Written by Jana Buch
Translated by Sarah Herndon and Jana Buch

[1] Direct quote of the word Arisa says in the video “ใช่” which translates to “yes” or “that’s true”

The form densifies
sweltering and liquid
The head in his left hand
Pride in his eyes

His gaze, focus driven,
sketches a concept of the duplicate
The spirit of the master's touch
once shaped hair by hair

Eyes and hands
mold the bodies
the body
without a . . . .

Negative and positive
In one cast
The details are now lost
"True"[1]

Brute embrace
Cut and shot right through the center
The highest of Gods
are looking down upon me

Mistranslation
of a language without sound
It only knows gestures
Still I hear it every day

I sense
I know
I'm warning
I'm . . . .

My will
is hanging from the tree
Just like my breast:
I will take them down later

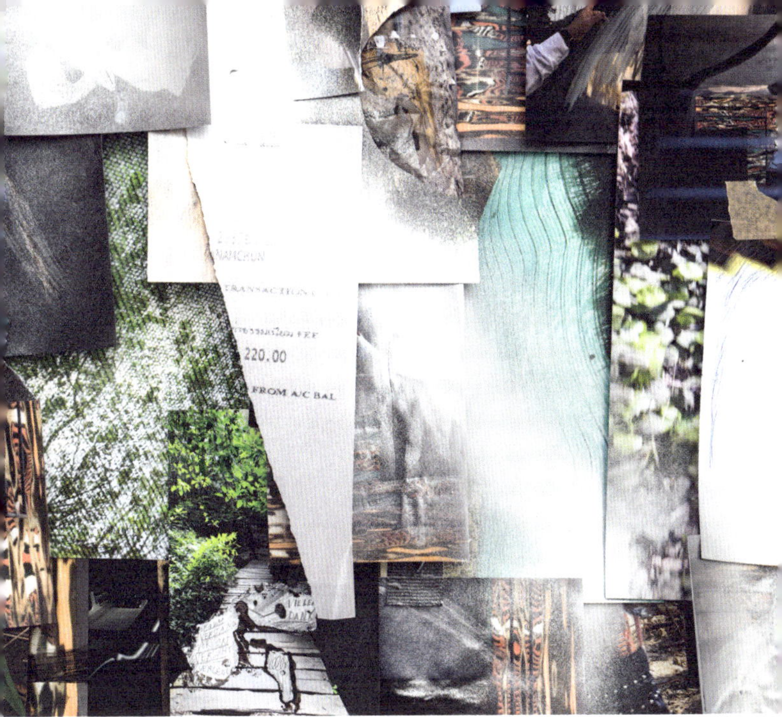
220.00
FROM A/C BAL

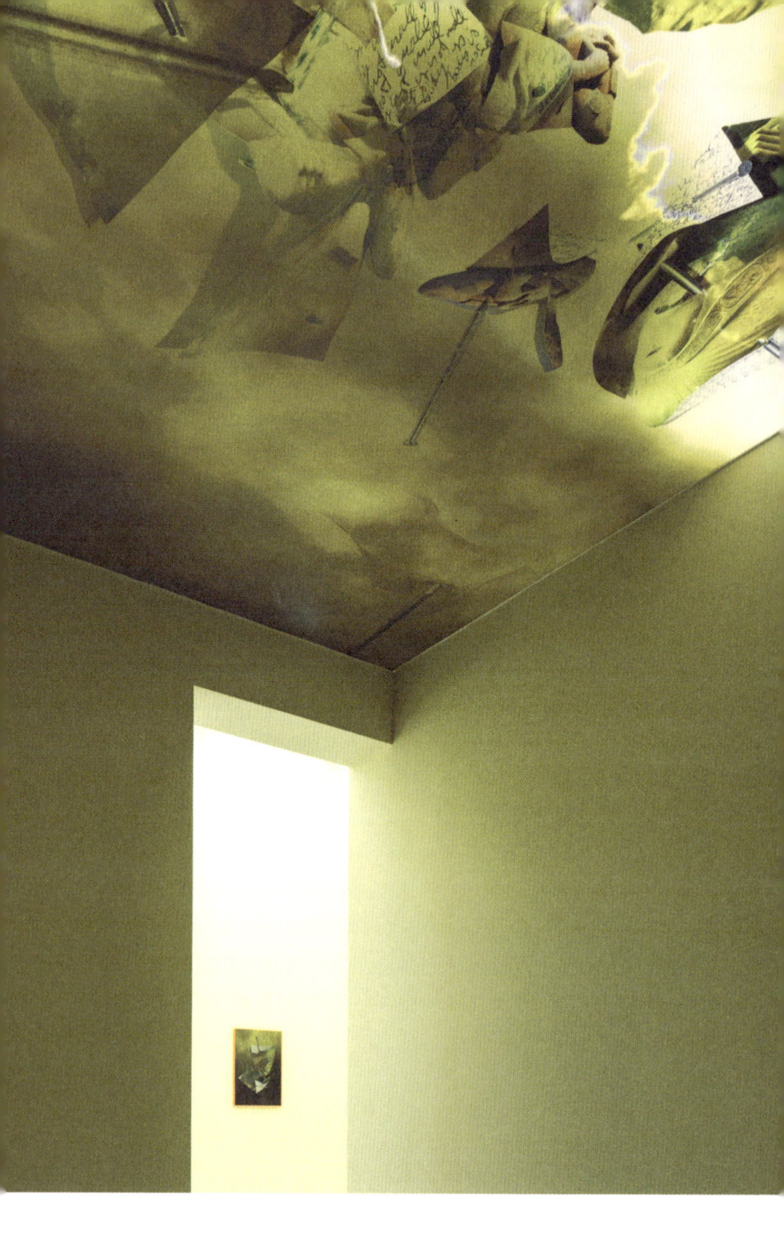

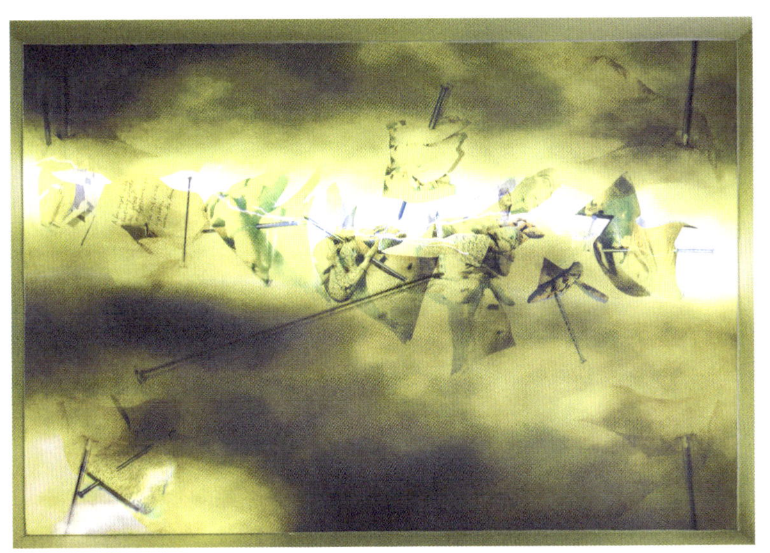

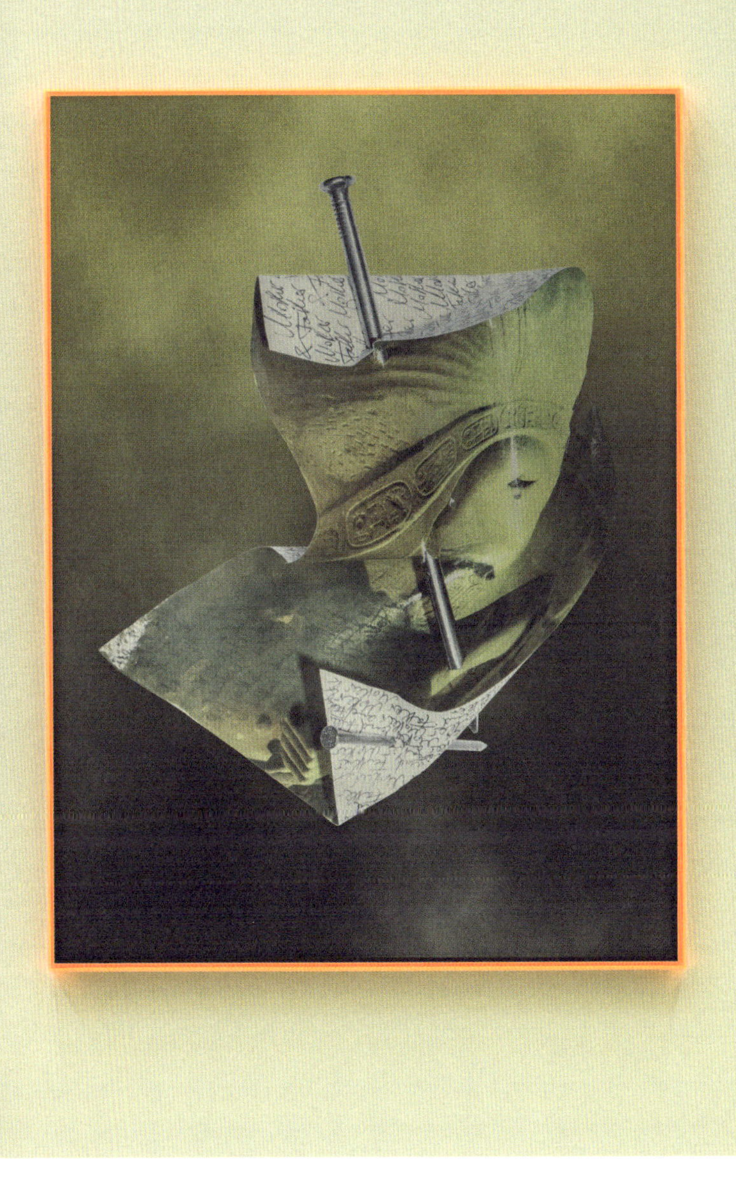

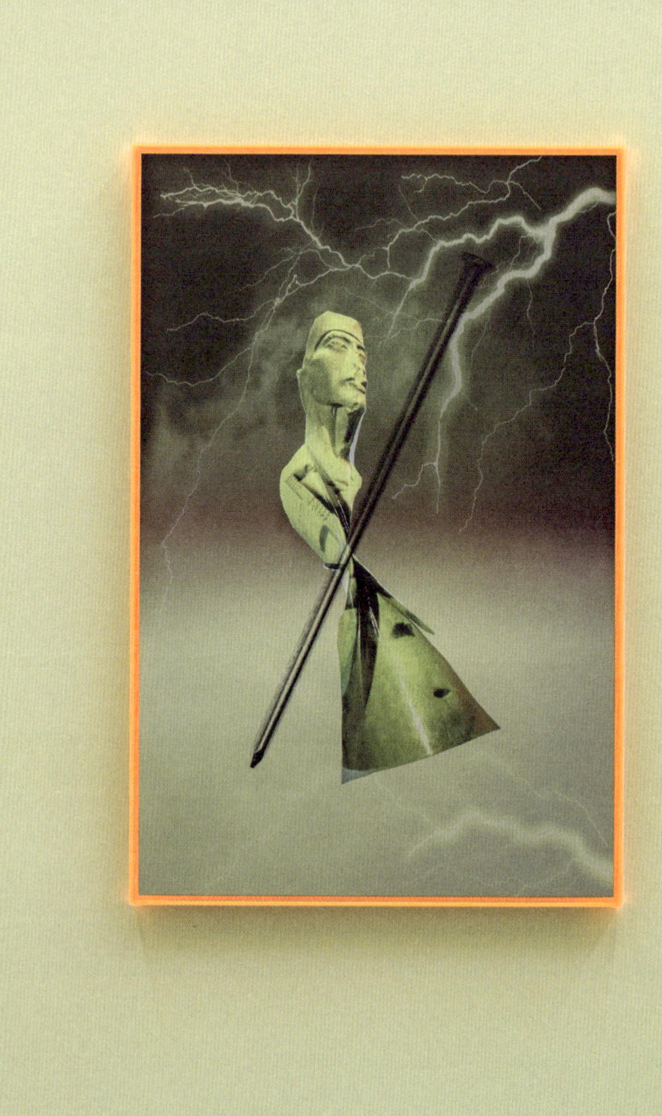

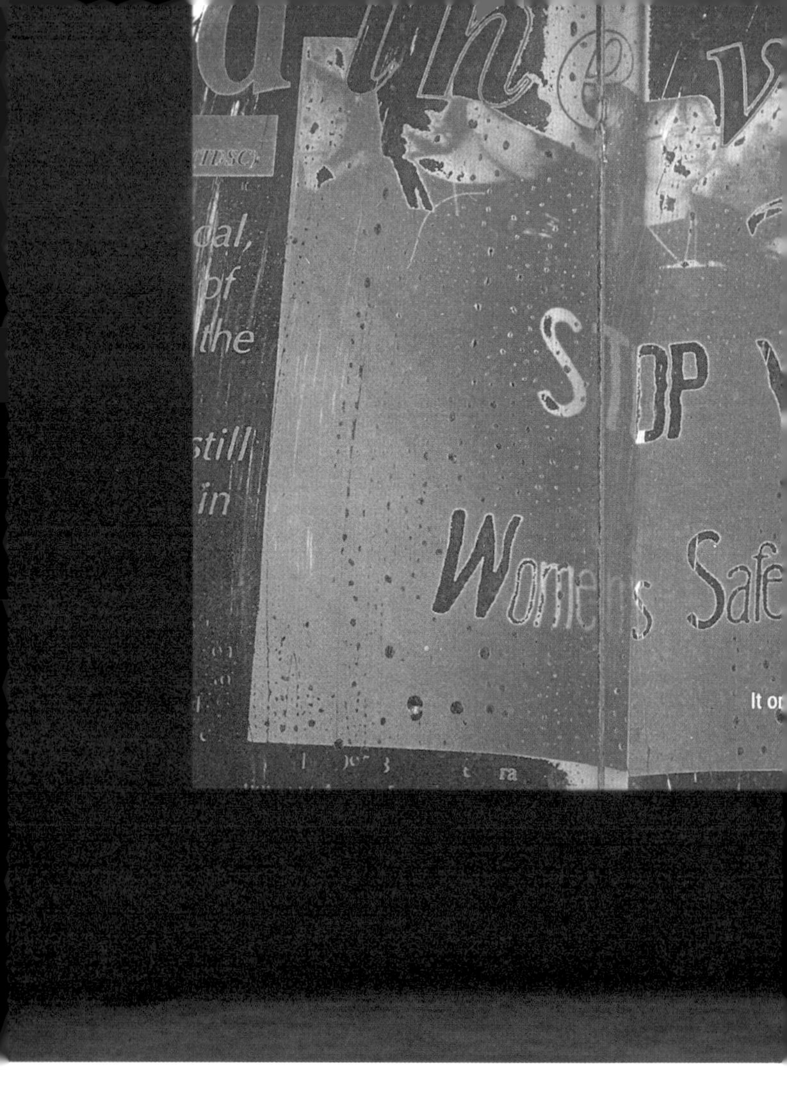

the
still
in

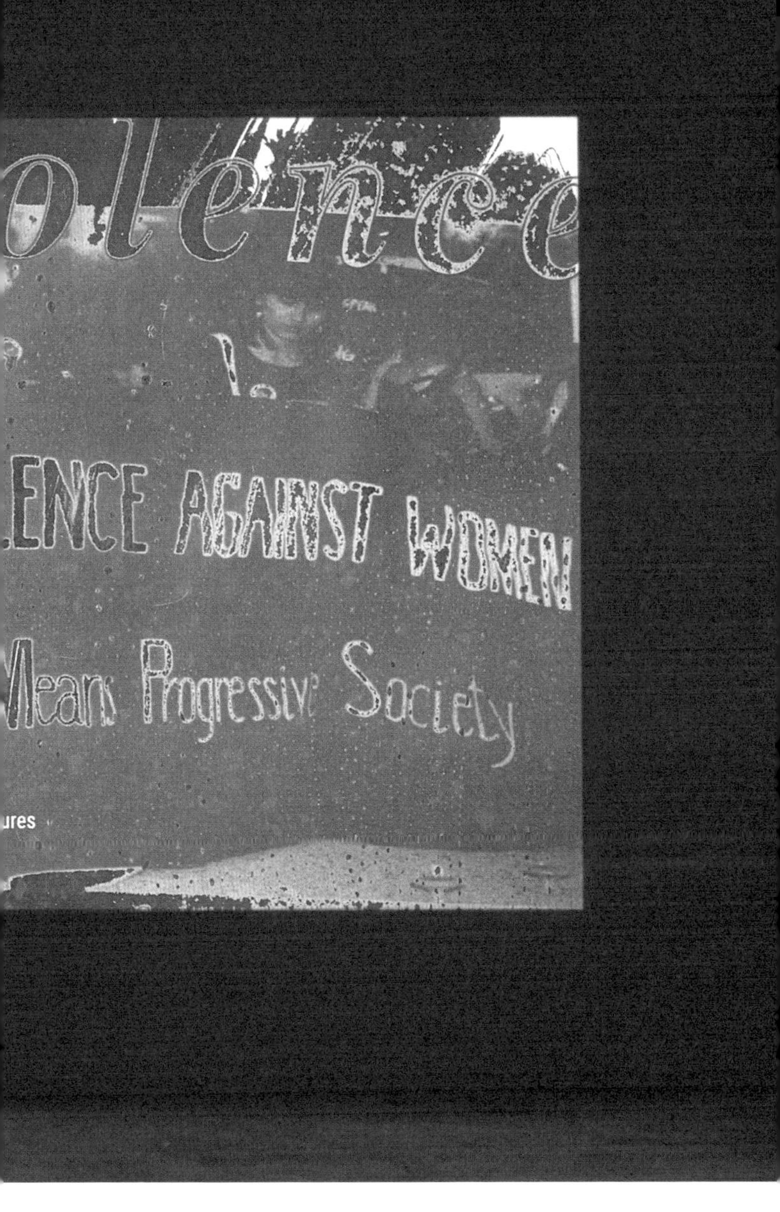
olence
LENCE AGAINST WOMEN
Means Progressive Society
ures

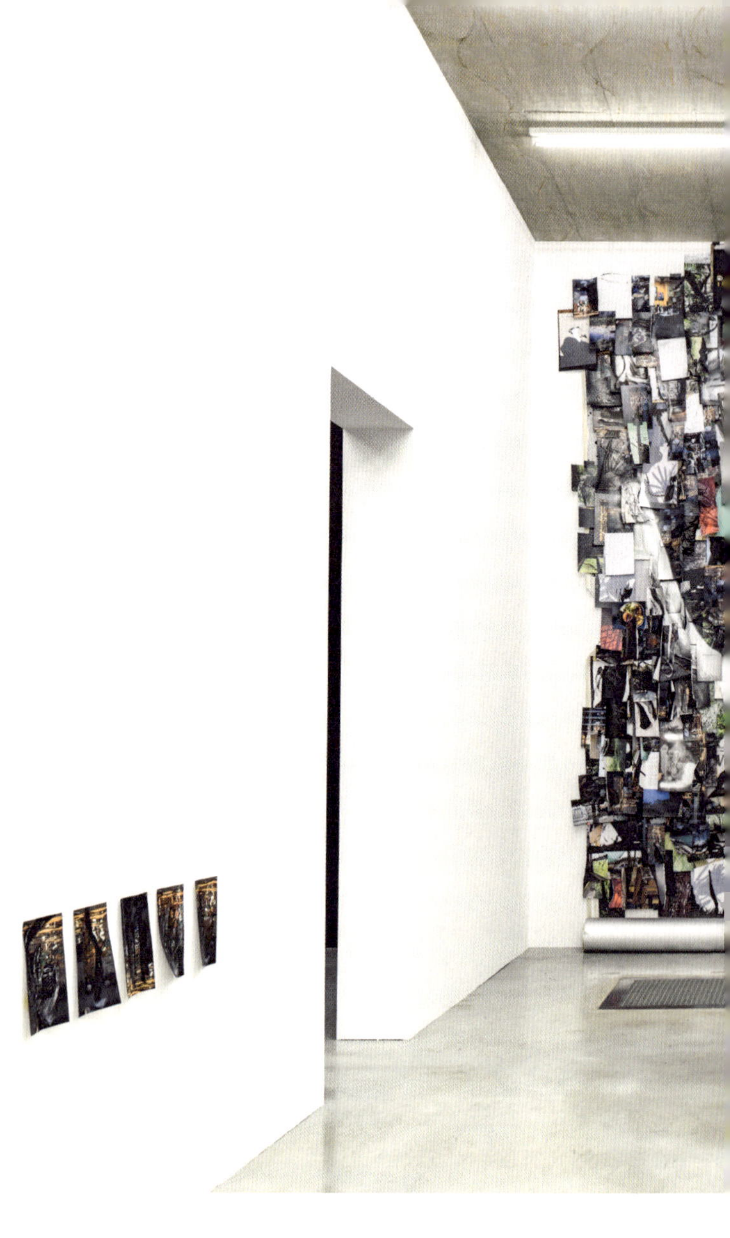

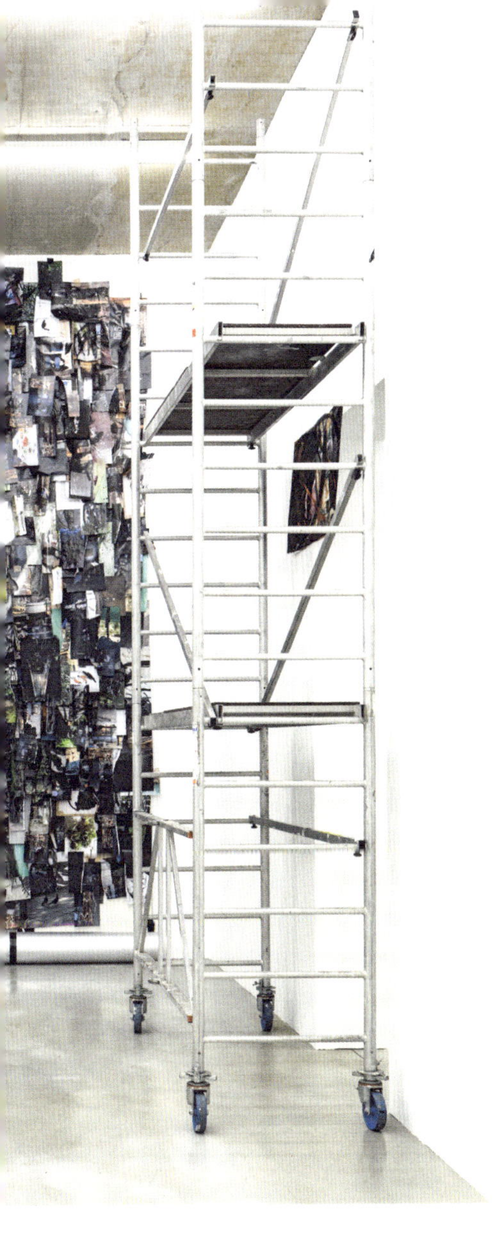

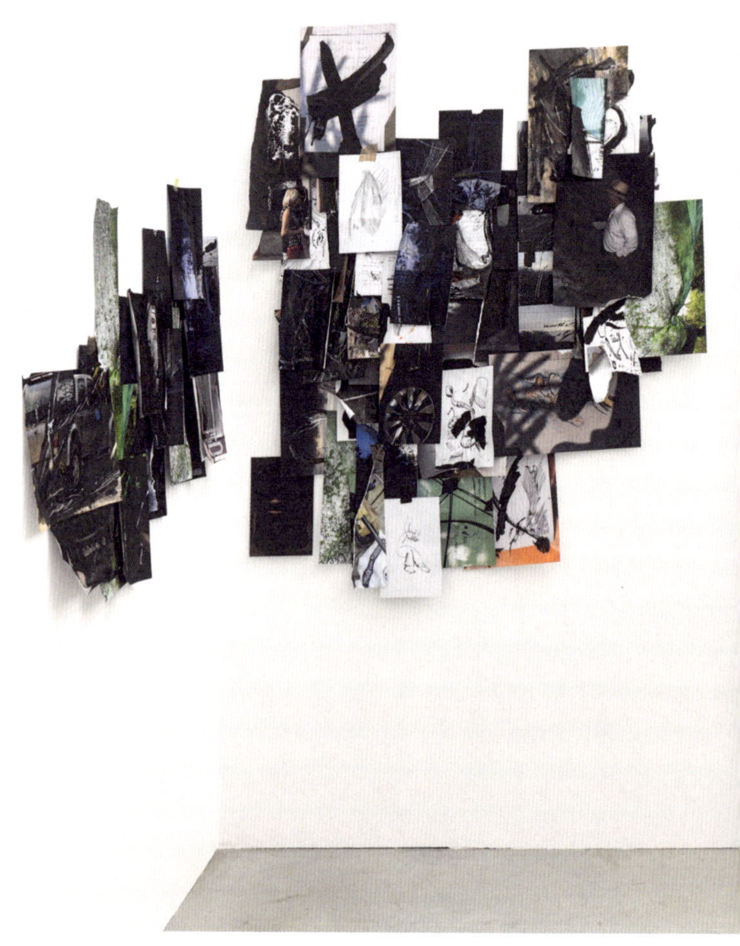

Arisa Purkpong

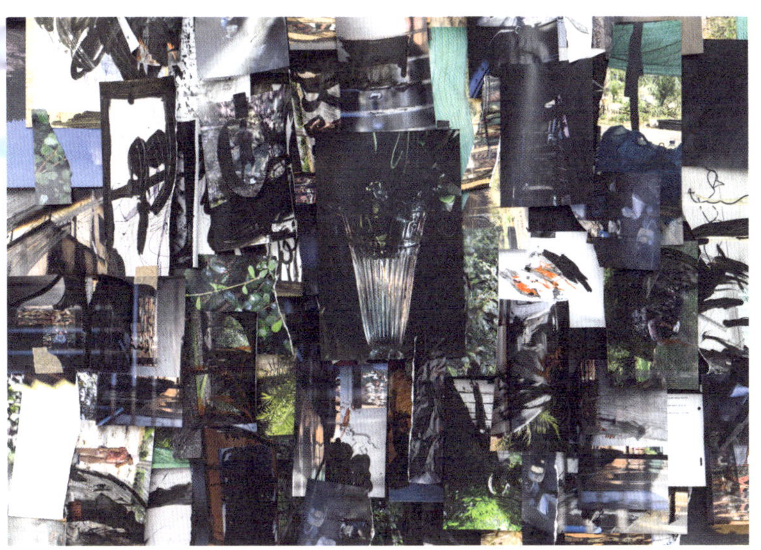

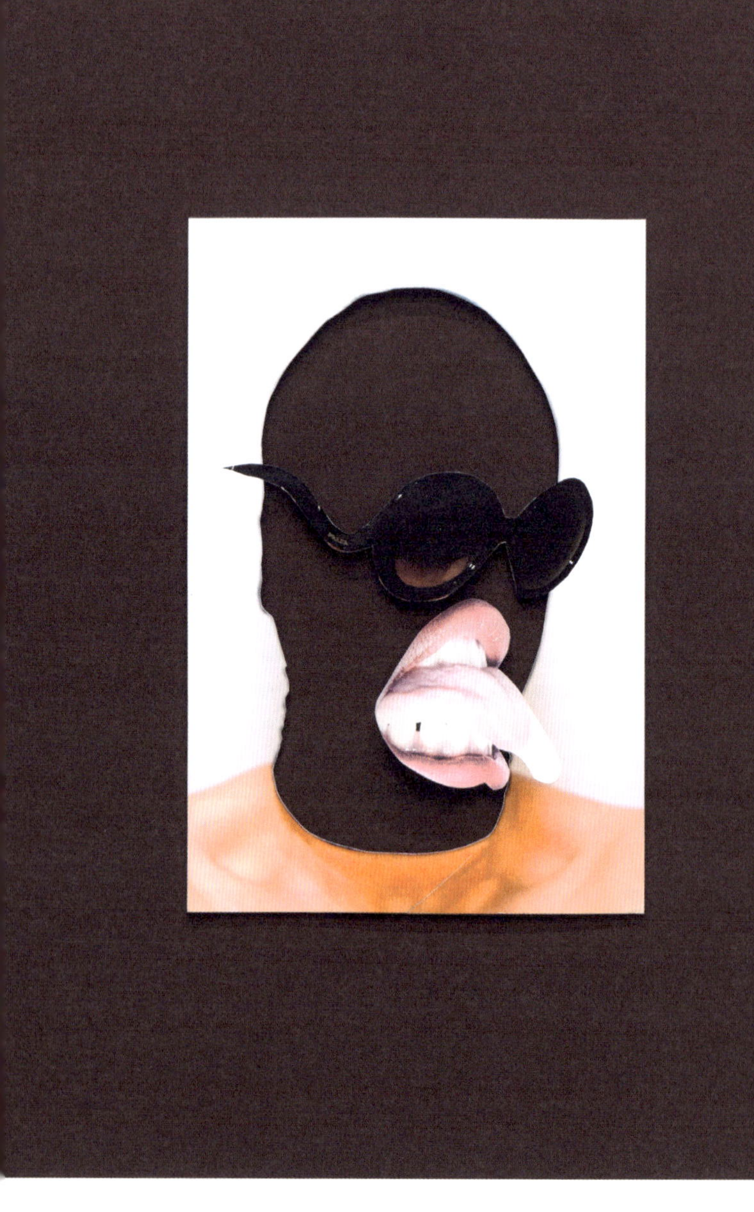

Anys Reimann

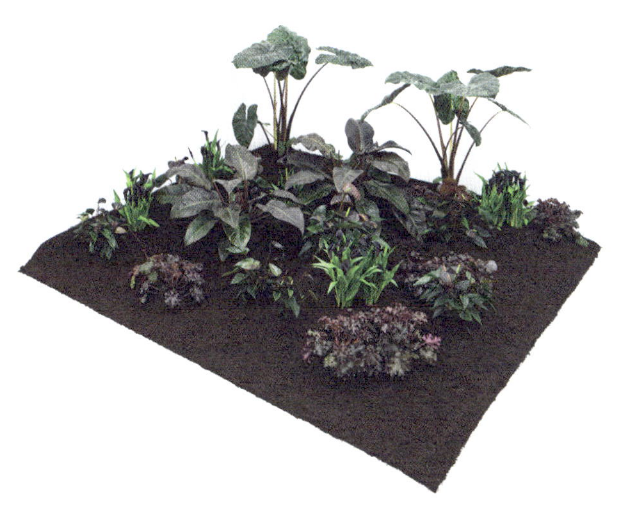

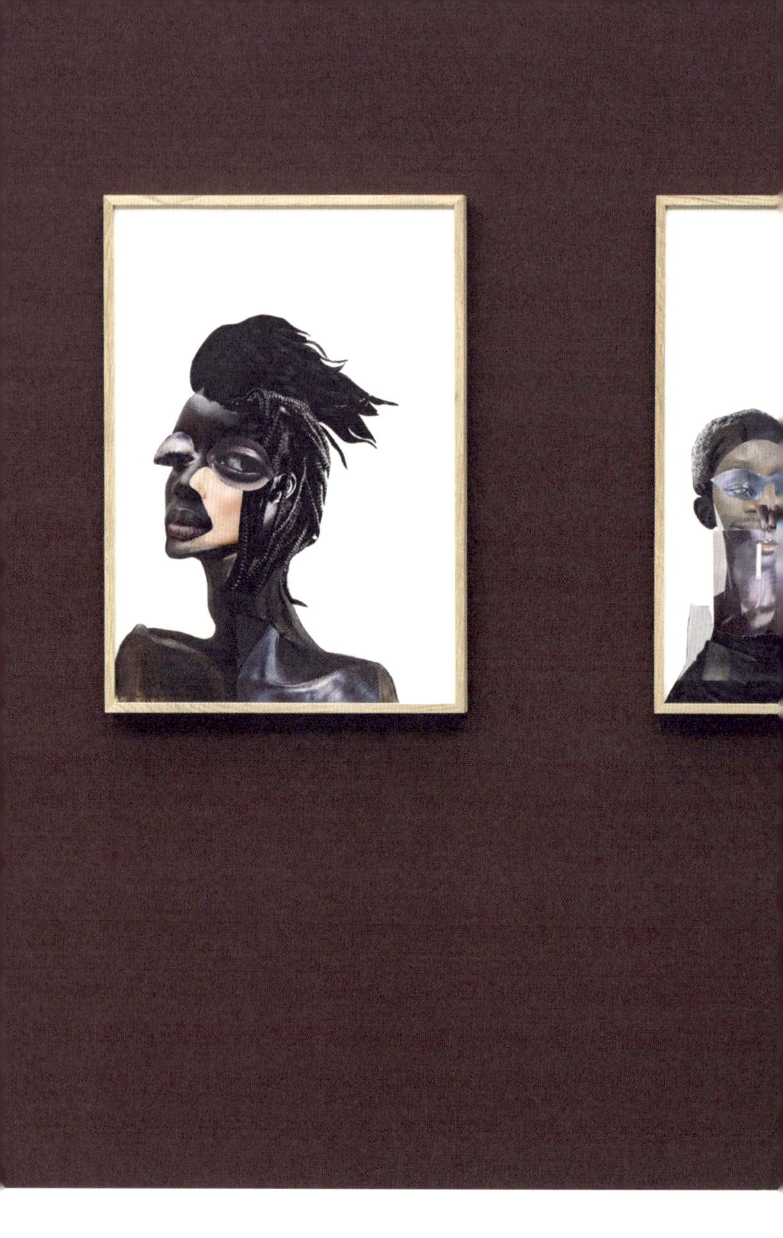

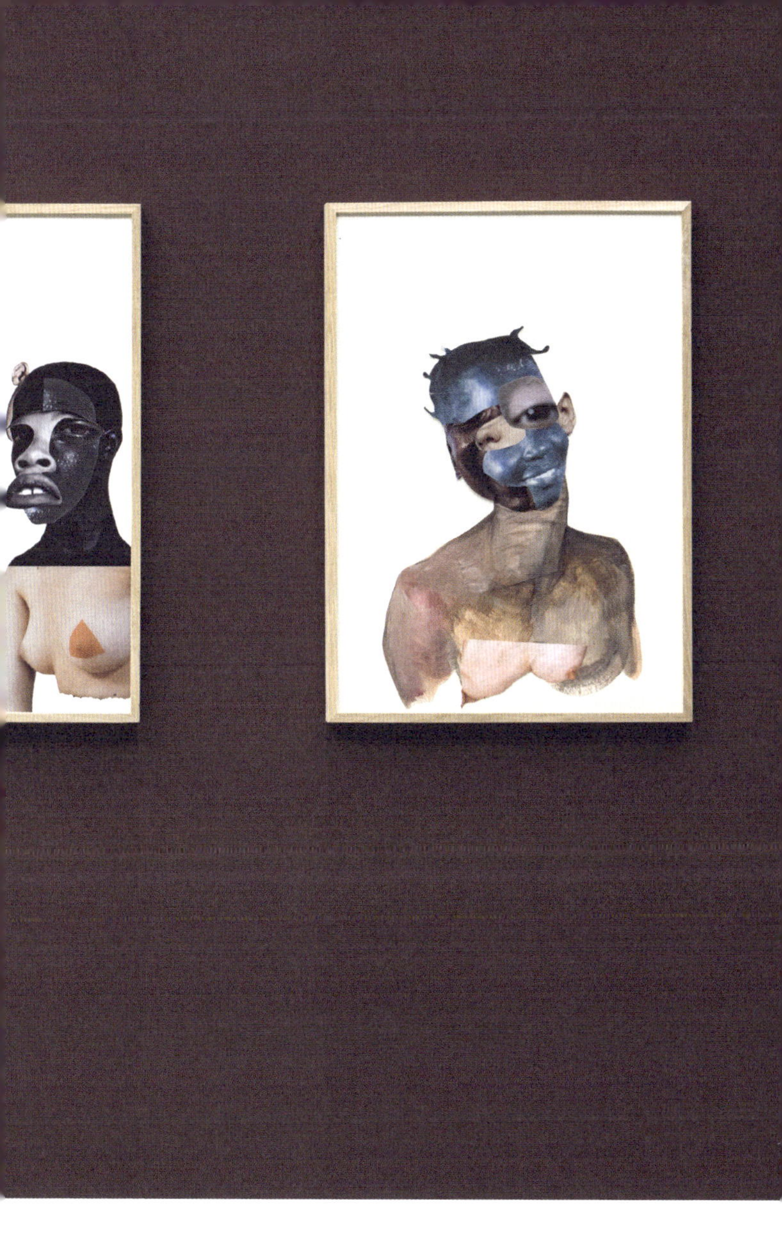

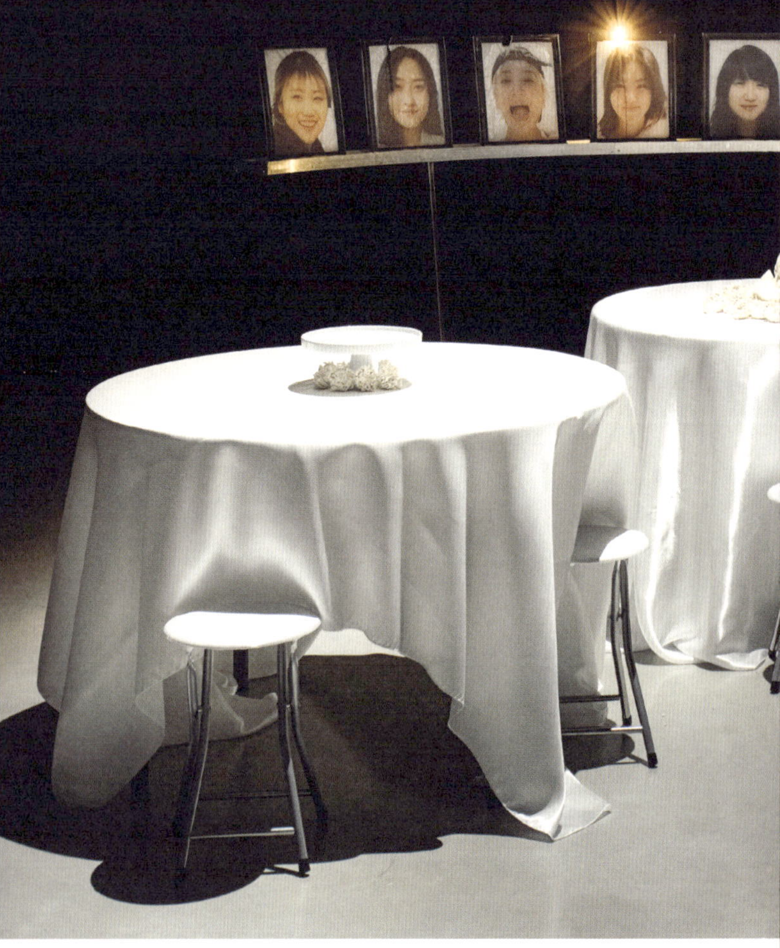

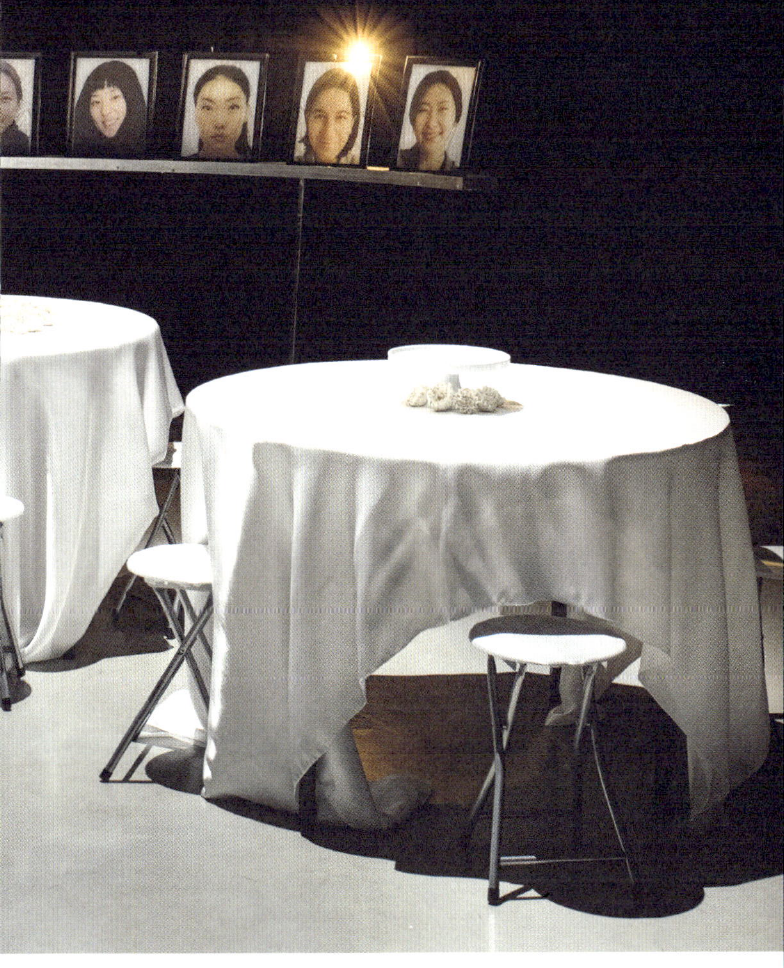

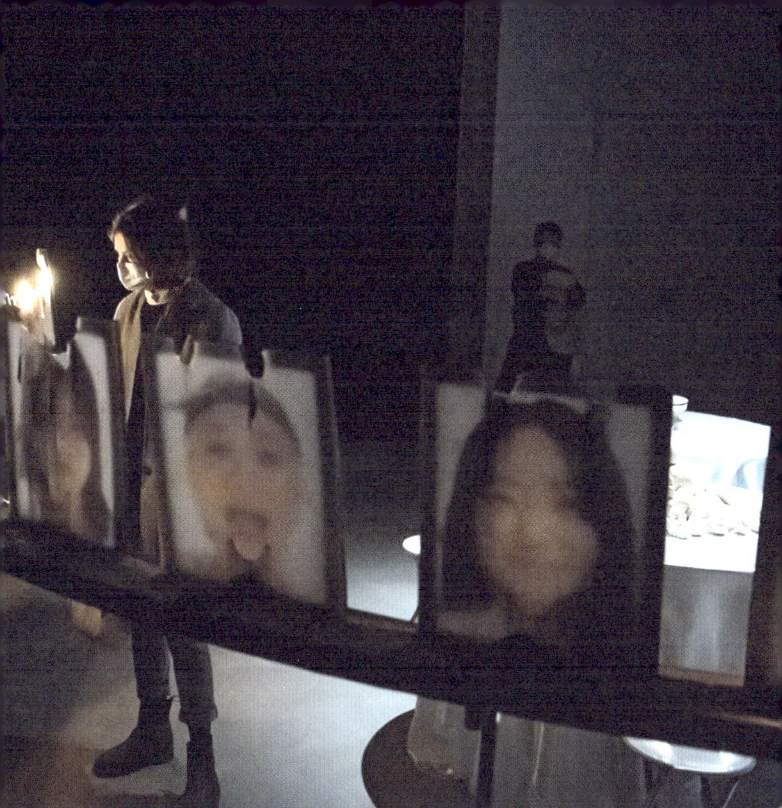

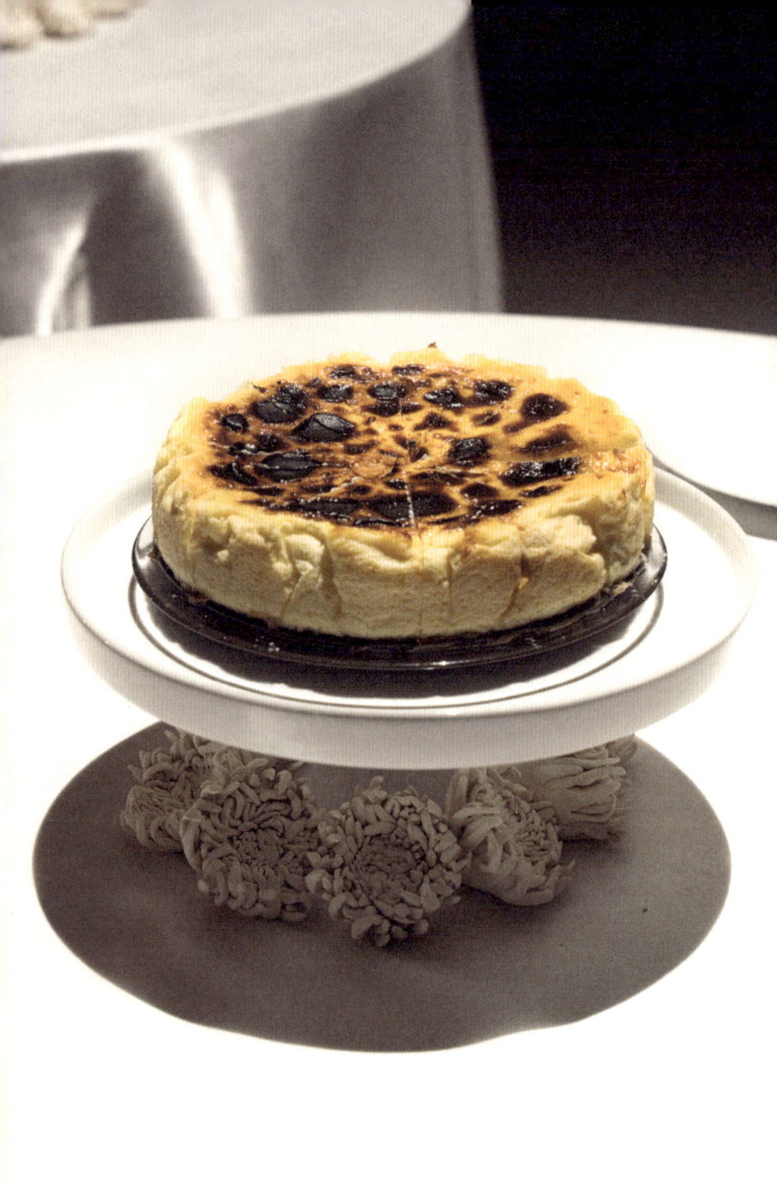

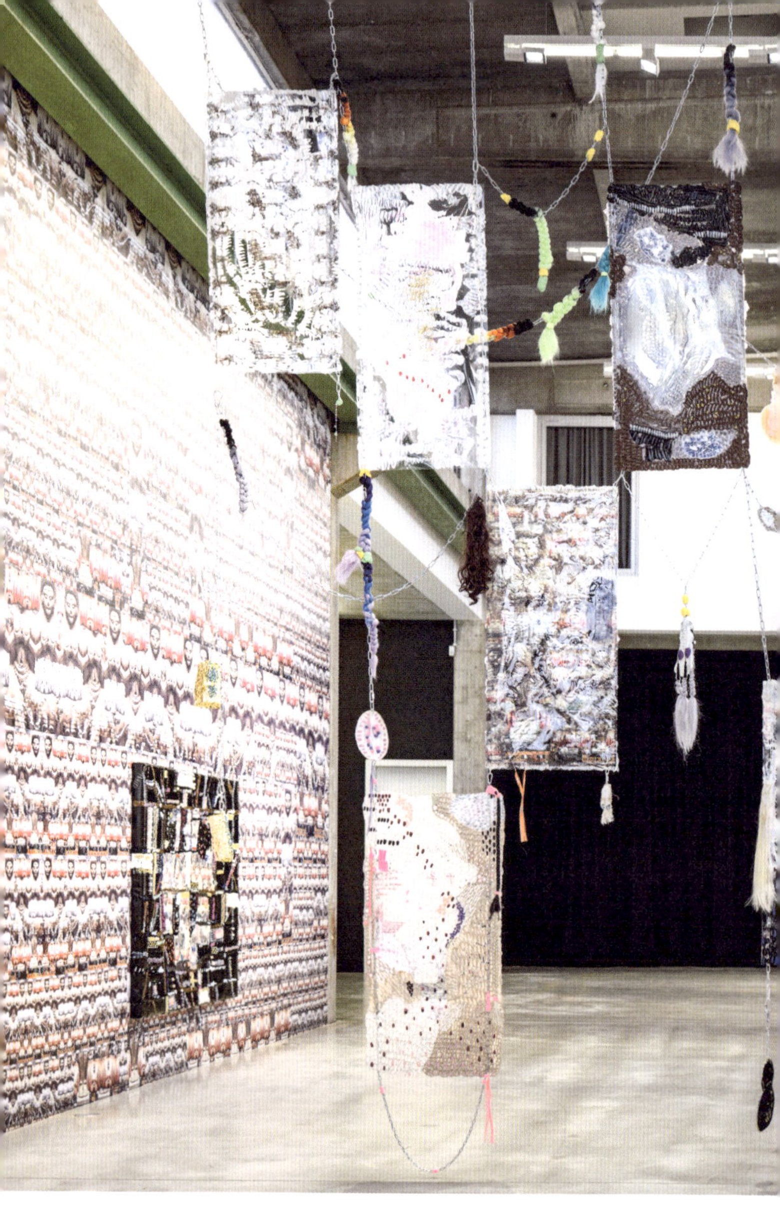

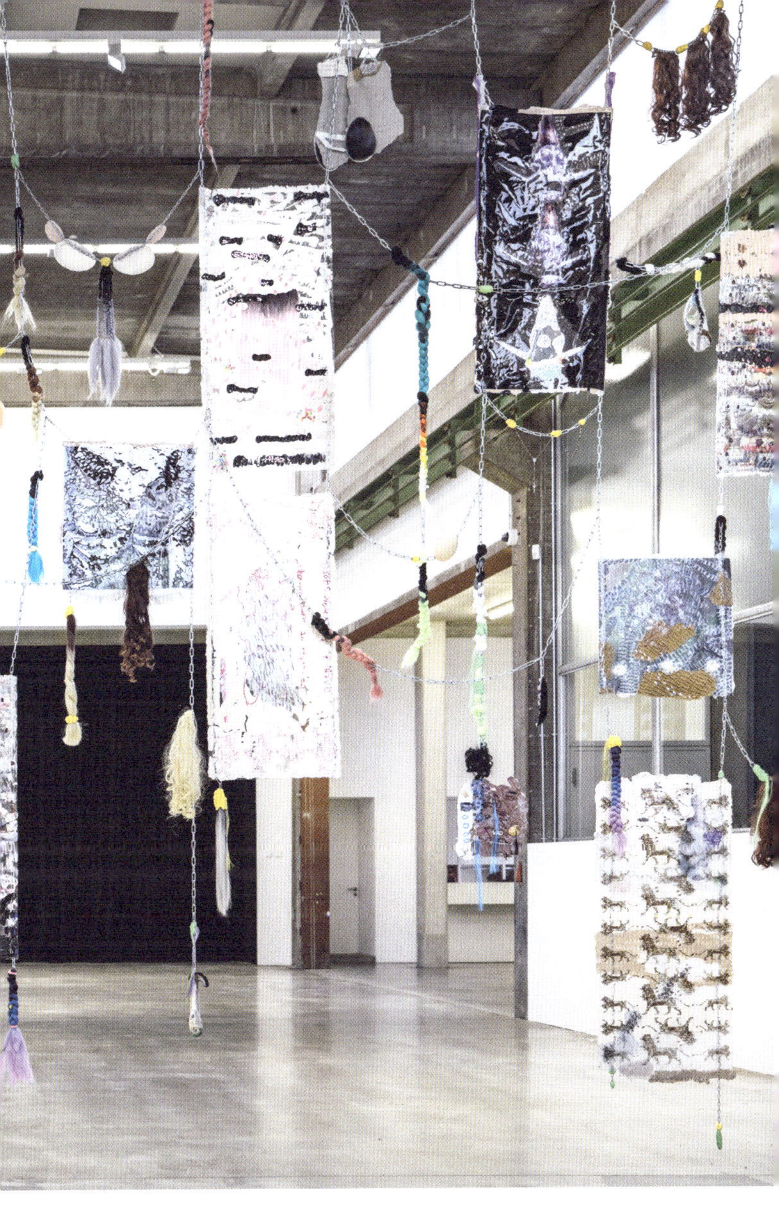

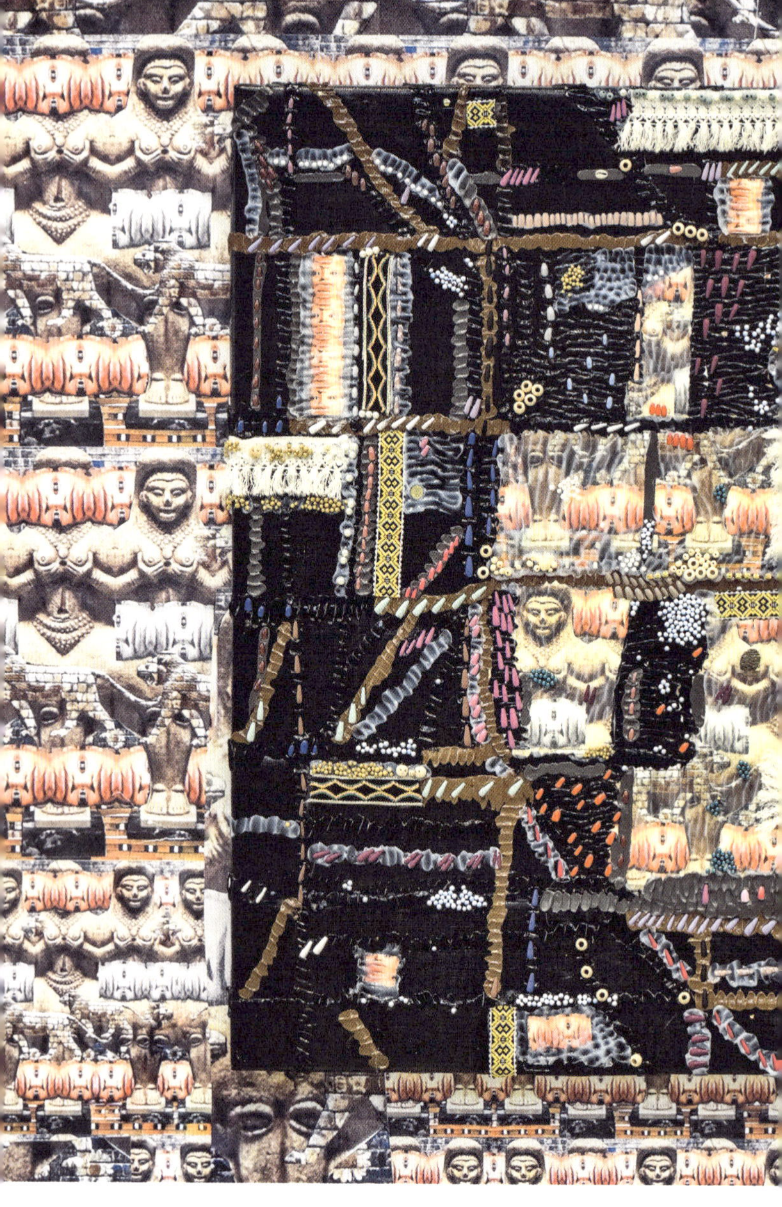

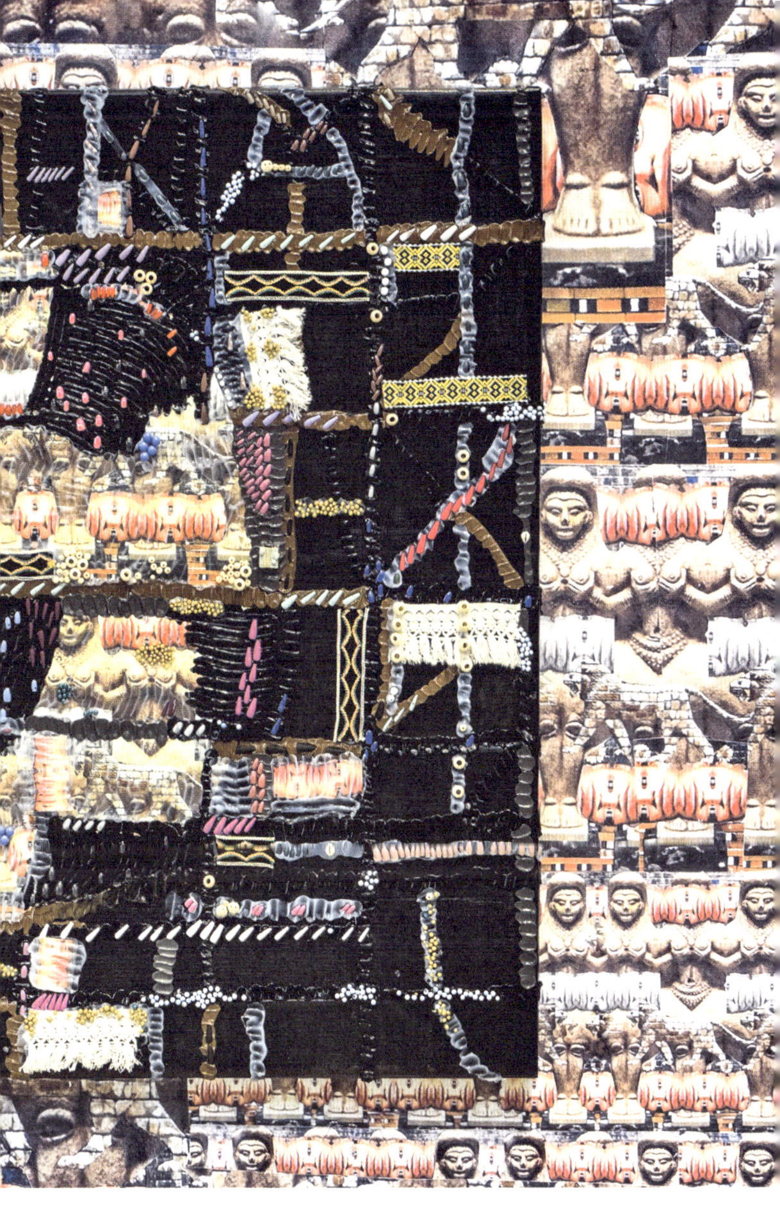

19, 69
Nara Bak
So wachet nun, weil ihr den Tag nicht wisset noch die Stunde
2021
Wachsporträts von | Wax portraits of: Areumbit Park, Seoyoung Yun, Jang Jung Yun, Arisa Purkpong, Kyounghyun Min, Eunbi Oh, Lauraine Mak, Laude Yu, Yuni Hwang, Chaelin Jeon
Je | Each 40 × 30 cm
Leihgabe der Künstler*in | Courtesy of the artist

23, 56–57
Jana Buch & Arisa Purkpong
Notizen aus Stein
2020
Video
8' 31''
Idee und Bilder | Concept and images: Jana Buch & Arisa Purkpong
Musik | Music: Tim Löhde
Stimme | Voice: Elena Packhäuser
Lektorat | Copyediting: Sarah Herndon & Lóa Aðalheiður Kristínardóttir
Leihgabe der Künstlerinnen | Courtesy of the artists

27
Donja Nasseri
Feminity Photography
2021
Fotografie auf gebürstetem Aluminium, Acrylrahmen | Photography on brushed aluminum, acrylic frame
120 × 87 cm
Leihgabe der Künstlerin | Courtesy of the artist

31, 49, 58–61
Arisa Purkpong
Ohne Titel | Untitled
2021
Papier, Laserdruck, Tintenstrahldruck, Tusche, Bleistift, Kugelschreiber, Sprühfarbe, Klebeband | Paper, laser print, inkjet print, ink, pencil, biro pen, spray paint, adhesive tape
Maße variabel | Dimensions variable
Leihgabe der Künstlerin | Courtesy of the artist

35
Anys Reimann
BLACK PLATEAU
2020
Collage aus Papier und Farbe | Paper and paint collage
120 × 86 cm
Leihgabe der Künstlerin | Courtesy of the artist

39, 72–73
Theresa Weber
Transformation Gate (Detail)
2021
Verschiedene Materialien | Mixed media
Dimensionen variabel | Dimensions variable
Leihgabe der Künstlerin | Courtesy of the artist

50–51
Donja Nasseri
A Great Deal of Controversy
2021
Print auf Stoffgewebe | Print on fabric
5,2 × 3,7 m
Leihgabe der Künstlerin | Courtesy of the artist

53
Donja Nasseri
Great Deal of Controversy 1
2021
Fotografie auf gebürstetem Aluminium, Acrylrahmen | Photography on brushed aluminum, acrylic frame
80 × 60 cm
Leihgabe der Künstlerin | Courtesy of the artist

54
Donja Nasseri
A Great Deal of Controversy 5
2021
Fotografie auf gebürstetem Aluminium, Acrylrahmen | Photography on brushed aluminum, acrylic frame
60 × 40 cm
Leihgabe der Künstlerin |
Courtesy of the artist

62
Anys Reimann
Ohne Titel (a Self) | Untitled (a Self)
2021
Collage aus Fotografie und Papier |
Photography and paper collage
29,7 × 21 cm
Leihgabe der Künstlerin |
Courtesy of the artist

63
Anys Reimann
SCHWARZER GARTEN
2021
Pflanzen (Calla, Heuchera, Anturium „Schoko", Alaucasia, Phillodendron), Erde |
Plants (Calla, Heuchera, Anturium "Choco", Alaucasia, Phillodendron), soil
250 × 250 cm
Leihgabe der Künstlerin |
Courtesy of the artist

64–65
Anys Reimann
LE NOIR DE… I – III
2021
Collage aus Papier und Farbe |
Paper and paint collage
Je | Each 70 × 50 cm
Leihgabe der Künstlerin |
Courtesy of the artist

66–67
Nara Bak
Trauercafé
2021
Soundarbeit mit | Sound piece with:
Arisa Purkpong, Stimme: Elena Packhäuser, Nara Bak, Jana Buch, Jihye Lee,
Text: Jana Buch, Nara Bak, Jihye Lee
Leihgabe der Künstler*in |
Courtesy of the artist

70
Nara Bak
Trauercafé
2021
Performance mit Kuchen |
Performance with cake
29.10.2021, 20. & 21.11.2021, 18. & 19.12.2021, 22. & 23.01.2022
Leihgabe der Künstler*in |
Courtesy of the artist

74–75
Theresa Weber
Ishtar Wallpaper
2020
Foliendruck auf Wand | Foil print on wall
5,5 × 16 m
Leihgabe der Künstlerin |
Courtesy of the artist

Theresa Weber
Hybrid
2021
Silikon und Collage auf PVC |
Silicone and collage on PVC
160 × 200 cm
Leihgabe der Künstlerin |
Courtesy of the artist

Sammlung Philara
Birkenstraße 47a
40233 Düsseldorf
www.philara.de
info@philara.de

Öffnungszeiten | Opening Hours
FR 14–20 Uhr
SA 14–18 Uhr
SO 14–18 Uhr
Pay what you wish

Direktion | Director
Katharina Klang

Kuratorin | Curator
Julika Bosch

Sammlungsbetreuung, Registrar |
Collection Management, Registrar
Ruben Benjamin Smulczynski

Wissenschaftliche Mitarbeit |
Research Fellow
Hannah Niemeier

Vermittlung | Guided Tours
Simon Ertel, Estira Memet, Naomi Röers

Eventmanagement | Event Managment
Benita von Puttkamer

Empfang | Front Desk
Christina Brikmann, Sonja Heim, Maxi Lorenz

Ausstellungstechnik | Technical Team
Frederic Bahr, Nico Flies, Sonja Heim, Min-Hae Sohn

Haustechnik | Building Services
Kalle Lenders

Licht-, Ton- und Videotechnik |
Lights, Sound and Video
Fred Flor

Design
Laura Catania, Thomas Artur Spallek

Dieser Katalog erscheint anlässlich der Ausstellung | This catalogue is published on the occasion of the exhibition

Attempts to Be Many
Nara Bak, Jana Buch, Donja Nasseri, Arisa Purkpong, Anys Reimann, Theresa Weber
30. Oktober 2021 – 23. Januar 2022
30 October, 2021 – 23 January, 2022

Herausgeberinnen | Editors
Julika Bosch, Katharina Klang, Sammlung Philara

Kuratorinnen der Ausstellung | Curators of the Exhibition
Julika Bosch, Katharina Klang

Idee | Concept
Katharina Klang

Wissenschaftliche Mitarbeit | Research Fellow
Hannah Niemeier

Autorinnen | Authors
Julika Bosch
Jana Buch
Katharina Klang
Mithu Sanyal

Lektorat | Editing
Kristina Helena Pavićević

Übersetzung | Translation
Barbara Lang

Gestaltung | Design
Studio Thomas Spallek

Gesamtherstellung | Production
Druckerei Kettler, Bönen

Erschienen im | Published by
Verlag Kettler, Dortmund

ISBN 978-3-98741-008-6

Abbildungsnachweis | Photo Credits
Alle Fotos, wenn nicht anders angegeben | All photos, if not mentioned otherwise:

Foto | Photo: Kai Werner Schmidt

Foto, S. | Photo, p. 19: Nara Bak
Foto, S. | Photo, p. 39: Johannes Bendzulla
Foto, S. | Photo, p. 69: Katja Illner
Foto, S. | Photo, p. 70: Jana Buch

Dank | Acknowledgements
Familie Bronner | Bronner Family